D0651419

Presented to the
Tulsa City-County Library
by

tulsa
LIBRARY TRUST

MAR   2023

CONVICTION

CONVICTION

The Murder Trial That Powered
Thurgood Marshall's Fight for Civil Rights

DENVER NICKS AND JOHN NICKS

Lawrence Hill Books

Chicago

Copyright © 2019 by Denver Nicks and John Nicks
All rights reserved
Published by Lawrence Hill Books
An imprint of Chicago Review Press Incorporated
814 North Franklin Street
Chicago, Illinois 60610
ISBN 978-1-61373-833-7

Library of Congress Cataloging-in-Publication Data
Names: Nicks, Denver, author. | Nicks, John, 1952– author.
Title: Conviction : the murder trial that powered Thurgood Marshall's
    fight for civil rights / Denver Nicks and John Nicks.
Description: Chicago, Illinois : Lawrence Hill Books, [2019] | Includes
    index.
Identifiers: LCCN 2018044427 (print) | LCCN 2018044977 (ebook) | ISBN
    9781613738344 (pdf) | ISBN 9781613738351 (kindle) | ISBN
    9781613738368 (epub) | ISBN 9781613738337 (cloth)
Subjects: LCSH: Lyons, Willie D. (W. D.)—Trials, litigation, etc. | Trials
    (Murder)—Oklahoma. | Murder—Investigation—Oklahoma. | African
    Americans—Civil rights—Oklahoma—History. | Race discrimination—
    Law and legislation—United States—History. | Civil rights—United
    States—History. | Marshall, Thurgood, 1908–1993.
Classification: LCC KF224.L96 (ebook) | LCC KF224.L96 N53 2019 (print)
    | DDC 345.766/02523—dc23
LC record available at https://lccn.loc.gov/2018044427

Typesetting: Nord Compo

Printed in the United States of America
5 4 3 2 1

For Linda

Yes! there's a limit to the despot's power!
When the oppressed looks round in vain for justice,
When his sore burden may no more be borne,
With fearless heart he makes appeal to Heaven,
And thence brings down his everlasting rights,
Which there abide, inalienably his,
And indestructible as are the stars.
—Friedrich Schiller, *William Tell*, 1804

A NOTE ON SOURCES

THE STORY RECOUNTED in these pages is drawn from many different sources, some more reliable than others. They include contemporary newspaper accounts, previously published books and academic articles, interviews with individuals directly connected to the people or events described herein, transcripts of court proceedings, correspondence between the individuals described in these events, the authors' observations of people and places, and, in rare cases, the authors' inference regarding what seems reasonable or obvious in the context of events (for instance, that a bailiff—a grown man—would bend down to allow an eight-year-old boy to reach a bible while being sworn in as a witness).

The transcript of court proceedings has been reproduced faithfully with minor corrections for spelling and punctuation, when such corrections don't alter the facts or tone of the speaker or of the proceedings. In reproducing the court's account of proceedings, we have left out some testimony and some long lines of questioning where they become tedious, do not advance the narrative (for instance, questions asked to establish the precise geographic location of one building in relation to another), or are not germane to the story. We have also, at times, left out some questions and answers between the attorneys and witnesses in cases where questions are intentionally redundant to keep a clear record for the court. For instance, this exchange:

"They were burned?"

"Yes."

"All of them burned?"

"Yes."

"Where did you take them?"

has been shortened to:

"They were burned?"

"Yes."

"Where did you take them?"

In rare cases, we have combined questions or answers to clarify and reduce redundancy as well. For instance, this exchange:

"Did you see W.D. Lyons in the Quarters that day?"

"Do you mean New Year's day?"

"Yes."

has been shortened to:

"Did you see W.D. Lyons New Year's day?"

The correspondence reprinted here is not a complete record but a selection of key pieces of correspondence from the major figures in this story. The correspondence has been reproduced faithfully, with minor corrections in spelling and punctuation when such corrections are necessary for the sake of clarity and do not alter the facts or tone of the correspondent. Because his letters are a unique window into the inner life of a central player, correspondence from W.D. Lyons has been reproduced verbatim to the greatest extent possible. Sections of correspondence that are redundant or unconnected to these events have been left out.

As is plainly evident from our reading and use of these sources, we believe W.D. Lyons's account of events to be the truth.

PROLOGUE

June 23, 1865
Fort Towson, Indian Territory

THE GENERAL WAS not in good spirits as he rode with his men toward Fort Towson.

He'd been receiving dire news for weeks from other Confederate officers, as one after the next surrendered to Union forces, and from his wife too. For many months her tone had been bitter and weary as the tide in the war turned and chaos and lawlessness burned through Indian Territory. To escape the bedlam, she and the rest of the family fled south of the Red River, to Texas. Now she openly fretted that she'd had no word from him for more than a week while rumors churned that a price had been put on his head—or worse, that he'd already been captured. But before General Stand Watie could attend to his family, and to the formidable task of helping his devastated people sift through the ashes of their lives, he had somber business to attend. The war had split his people, the Cherokee Nation, into hateful factions—and his had lost. General Watie knew now that he would never return to life on his plantation as he'd known it. His slaves would be freed. Soon, he would collect his family and return home to rebuild with the daunting knowledge that the federal government of the United States would likely not look kindly on those who had joined the

Southern rebellion in defense of slavery. Their fight finished, Watie and his band of Native American soldiers for the Confederacy plodded on, surrounded by enemies, toward humiliation at best.

Months earlier, on April 9, 1865, General Lee had surrendered his army to Union forces at Appomattox, in Virginia. After that, the generals of the Confederacy laid down arms in waves undulating westerly through the Carolinas, Georgia, Alabama, Mississippi, Louisiana, and Arkansas. But in pockets on the periphery some stubbornly hung on, fighting skirmishes and raiding along the lawless outer rim of the Confederate States of America.

Watie was among those holdouts, resistant to the very end that he should be made to submit yet again to the government of the United States. He'd grown up in Georgia, the son of a wealthy, slave-owning, full-blood Cherokee father and a half-white mother. Though his family enjoyed a position of prominence among the Cherokee political elite, they were forced like the others from their land by a federal government largely disinclined and helpless to stop the torrent of settlers illegally encroaching on territory the tribe had been promised into perpetuity. Watie resettled his family west of the Mississippi River, in the Indian Territory set aside for the tribes on the far side of the Ozark Mountains. He'd started anew, running a successful plantation on the labor of black slaves. He prospered there, until it began to look as though the government in Washington intended to end slavery throughout the country, and the states of the South declared their independence. Watie, like most other Native Americans expelled from their ancestral homes to Indian Territory, whether Cherokee, Chickasaw, Creek, Seminole, or Choctaw, had little reason to feel affinity toward the United States of America, so he joined in the Southern cause.

Now, that cause was lost.

On June 23, 1865, Watie and his lonely band of Confederates rode into Doaksville, a small settlement adjacent to an old frontier outpost called Fort Towson, in the Choctaw Nation, near where the Kiamichi flows into the Red River in the lowlands at the foothills of the Sans Bois Mountains. There, Stand Watie signed a formal cease-fire, becoming the last Confederate general to lay down arms at the close of the American Civil War.

1

December 31, 1939
Fort Towson, Choctaw County, Oklahoma

I T WAS COLD that Sunday night in Fort Towson, the town of around
five hundred that had grown up near the ruin of the old army
fort, along the railroad built in 1870 just south of the abandoned
Doaksville settlement.

First settled by French traders, outposts along the Red and
Kiamichi Rivers attracted the social outcasts and vagrants that
tended to congregate at the frontier, where law was scant and
where an abundance of diligence or a shortage of scruples could
yield a man a small fortune. In 1824, the United States established
Fort Towson near the juncture of the two rivers to protect settlers
in western Arkansas from hostile Plains Indians and from the
threat of Mexican invasion. At the time that the fort was established at the far western frontier of a young United States, the
newly independent Republic of Mexico lay just on the far side of
the Red River a few miles to the south. The land soon became
the Choctaw Nation after the tribe became the first of many forc-
ibly removed from the southeastern United States and resettled
in Indian Territory in the 1830s. It was then used over time as
a staging ground for attacks on native tribes to the west, a commercial center and source of law and order for fur trappers and

settlers coming in from the east, a hub for the resettlement of the Choctaw and Chickasaw tribes, a staging ground for the US Army during the Mexican-American War, and, briefly, a Confederate headquarters during the Civil War. By 1939 the fort had long ago been abandoned and given back to the forest. But though it had been nearly a century since the military outpost had been put to any real use, the town that had blossomed in its shadow was alive and buzzing. Just fifteen miles down the highway was Hugo, the political and economic hub of Choctaw County.*

As in much of the country, and the world, the 1930s had been a disorienting and difficult decade for Oklahoma. The Great Depression, which devastated the global economy, hit particularly hard as a glut in oil production and the general economic decline sent petroleum prices tumbling—incomes in the state saw the third-greatest decline in the country. Decades of ill-advised and destructive farming practices had robbed huge tracts of the western plains of the prairie grasses that for eons had held the earth in place, and when drought struck, the wind picked up the topsoil and carried it away in monstrous clouds that blinded and choked farm animals, and some humans too, as the winds rumbled east across the continent. The Dust Bowl devastation sent pitiful throngs of refugees fleeing to safety in the west, toward California.

In eastern Oklahoma, commodity prices—especially for cotton—that had soared during the First World War tumbled in the 1920s and didn't rebound when the decade kicked over. Between 1935 and 1940, eighty thousand Oklahomans, many of

---

* Incidentally, the town Hugo was named for Victor Hugo, the Romantic-era French poet, novelist, and internationally renowned social justice activist. During his lifetime Hugo agitated relentlessly to abolish the death penalty, and his masterpiece novel *Les Misérables* is an epic condemnation of the brutality of poverty and a plea for prison reform.

them sharecroppers, fled the state, double or more the number of refugees from any other state in the union. One in six farmers was driven off the land, their abandoned farms snapped up by predatory mortgage and insurance companies and big-money landholders.

And yet, for all the economic hardship, life in Choctaw County trundled on, and by 1939 Hugo was on the cusp of a rebound, with a growing population of nearly six thousand and more than one hundred retail stores and restaurants. Fort Towson had two cotton gins, a few banks, and even two speakeasy beer joints—two more than the law allowed in officially dry Oklahoma. Though Prohibition at the federal level ended in 1933, Oklahomans would continue voting dry, as Okie humorist Will Rogers famously quipped, "as long as they can stagger to the polls." That day wouldn't come until 1959. The town hosted a large general store, where you could buy whiskey under the counter, and a fire department. A little passenger train known as "the dinky" traveled up and down the railroad that ran roughly parallel to Highway 70, stopping at each little town along the way between Hugo and Idabel. Neighbors knew each other by name, and many didn't even have locks on their doors, much less use them. If a passerby happened to be thirsty, it was commonplace to stop in at a neighbor's house and help oneself to a glass of water.

The state that began as a kind of concentration camp for indigenous tribes had become the land of opportunity for white and black settlers alike. After the Civil War, enslaved people in Indian Territory were set free, and over time more former slaves and their descendants moved to the state hoping to carve out a new future apart from the centuries of cruel servitude that had shaped life and culture in the Old South. Many of them succeeded, to a degree, establishing all-black towns like Boley, Rentiesville, and Langston. They found opportunity in pockets, but the racism of turn-of-the-century America ran deep in Oklahoma too. The first act of the Oklahoma legislature after achieving statehood in 1907 was to pass a law that defined anyone with any African ancestry as black and banned interracial marriage and interracial schools. Many of the same attitudes, Jim Crow laws, and racist cultural mores that characterized the Deep South prevailed in Oklahoma too. This was especially true in the state's southeastern quadrant, a region known colloquially as Little Dixie, with the strongest ties to the former Confederacy. The divisions and scars of racist oppression only deepened as Oklahoma's economy soured in the 1920s and '30s.

But on that Sunday night in 1939, residents of Choctaw County, black and white alike, celebrated.

Shortly after sunset a waning gibbous moon glowed over the snow-covered fields and forests surrounding Fort Towson, and the sounds of worshippers issued softly from the Holiness Church. Outside the church, people scuttled about the neighborhood, a small section on the west side of town of about a dozen black families' homes that residents called the Quarters and whites on the other side of town called the Nigger Quarters. They observed New Year's Eve modestly, talking and joking about this and that, or idling near the "troll bridge" that spanned the branch of what locals called Negro Creek, which ran through the community. Some were warm and tipsy, having taken the occasional swig throughout the day from a jug of moonshine, or "wildcat" as people called illegal whiskey in southeastern Oklahoma. Now and then, musicians in Donna Scott's Cafe would strike up a tune, sending music, fleetingly, into the cool evening air, like plumes of warm breath condensing in the cold. A long stretch of icy winter weather finally broke that Sunday, and for the first time in days the temperature rose mercifully above freezing. Just.

A twenty-one-year-old farmhand named Willie D. Lyons—known to his friends as W.D.—lived with his wife at his mother-in-law's house in Hugo, but on New Year's Eve he was in Fort Towson, where he had been raised. He spent a leisurely afternoon in and around the Quarters, hanging out with friends on the neighborhood's dirt streets, sometimes sneaking off to swig from a jug of wildcat hidden in the trees near the creek. He spent a while splitting wood for his wife and went rabbit hunting, without success, in the open pasture just beyond the thicket on the western boundary of the Quarters. As he meandered among the neighborhood's humble houses throughout the day, stopping for a hamburger at Donna Scott's Cafe, saying hello to friends and relatives, and finally turning in for the evening at his mother's house, he had with him a shotgun he'd borrowed from a friend. He carried the gun broken down into two parts, the barrel separated from the stock, with both pieces concealed furtively in newspaper. Lyons didn't have a hunting license.

Through the trees on the western perimeter of the Quarters, in the middle of the large field where Lyons had been hunting earlier that day, stood a ramshackle three-room farmhouse where Elmer and Marie Rogers lived with their three children. They were white sharecroppers and very poor, without money to buy window curtains for their sparse home or even enough chairs for the whole family to sit together at the dinner table.

As the moon rose over southeastern Oklahoma, while some in Fort Towson worshipped at church and others brought in the new year in their own fashion with family and friends, Elmer and Marie Rogers lay dead in their home. Elmer was prostrate on the floor between the two beds, surrounded by his own blood and shards of broken glass, his ribs full of buckshot, shattered and splintered, his skull crushed. Marie lay on the porch with a gunshot wound in her torso and her skull asunder. Her blood, brains, and the shattered pieces of her jaw were scattered about her corpse.

When the shooting started, Marie had yelled to her eldest son, seven-year-old James Glenn, to get the baby, Billie Don, and run. While he and his brothers hid in bed, James Glenn caught a glimpse of an intruder's hand in the darkness. After the men left, there was a tense quiet in the house while the children hid in terror, until the crackling and popping of wood set afire overtook the silence. Afraid that the four-year-old, Elvie Dean, would cry if he jostled him, and draw back the men who had murdered his parents, James Glenn grabbed the baby and ran.

Flames began to crawl out the windows of the house, lapping at the frigid nighttime air. Soon the entire structure ignited. The blaze, bright and orange against the flickering darkness, lit up the barren field. With the baby in his arms, a child carrying a child, James Glenn took off in a desperate sprint from the glowing inferno behind him. Down by the highway that ran east to Fort Towson and west to Hugo, he huddled in the cold near the road with his baby brother, stunned and terrified. A husband and wife from a few towns away who were driving west toward Hugo from Fort Towson spotted James Glenn by the highway. They stopped the car, doubled back, and saw that the boy had a baby with him. The couple loaded the children into the car and drove them back to Fort Towson. James Glenn's four-year-old brother, Elvie Dean, was still inside the house. He was burning alive.

———————

New Year's Day 1940 arrived frenetic and promising for Thurgood Marshall. The thirty-one-year-old Baltimore native was enjoying life in New York City as the new head lawyer for the National Association for the Advancement of Colored People as he prepared to try his first case before the US Supreme Court in just a few days' time. Founded in 1909, the NAACP was only a few years younger than Marshall himself, and by 1940 the group had matured into a powerful civil rights organization with real national reach worthy of its name.

Four years earlier, Marshall had moved from Baltimore to New York with his wife, Buster, to work full-time with the NAACP under the guidance of Charles Houston, his mentor and the former dean of Howard University Law School. In July 1938, Houston left New York, anxious to return home to his private practice in Washington, DC, and by 1939 Marshall was officially at the helm of the NAACP's legal office.

Like the organization for which he was now special counsel, the young lawyer still struggled to pay the bills—the promotion had included a small bump in pay of $200, bringing his meager salary to $2,600 a year, which he and Buster sometimes supplemented by delivering groceries for their Harlem co-op—but life in frenzied New York suited him. An energetic and affable bon vivant, Marshall relished Harlem's social life, dining and drinking often with friends, whom he regaled with stories of his frequent travels throughout the United States representing downtrodden clients and raising money for the cash-strapped NAACP. In the words of his former classmate at all-black Lincoln University, the poet Langston Hughes, Marshall was "good-natured, rough, ready and uncouth." A stark contrast to his predecessor Houston—a stony-faced former army officer—Marshall's jocular antics lit up the national office near Manhattan's Union Square, his towering, lanky frame and generous laugh bringing a welcome dose of levity to the vital work of battling the state-sponsored terrorism and systemic racist oppression that ruled over the lives of America's thirteen million black citizens.

Seismic changes in the way information was distributed and consumed across the country, like the widespread adoption of the radio, had created a new mass culture in the United States. Under the leadership of its ebullient national secretary, Walter White, the NAACP had become adept at influencing public opinion. Through public protests, the NAACP's national magazine *The Crisis*, and relationships with journalists around the country—most prominently among African American newspapers—White used his eye for drama and keen sense of an emerging pop culture in America to raise awareness of the plight of black Americans, especially in the South. White pressured companies, with some success, to drop the use of racist epithets in product names such as "Pickaninny Peppermints" and "Nigger Head Shrimp." Though southern Democrats in Washington blocked any legislation that would make lynching a federal offense and thus compel the federal government to prosecute perpetrators when state governments would not, the NAACP made substantial progress throughout the 1930s in waging a public opinion campaign to push back against the vigilantism and mob violence that terrorized black communities. Statistics compiled by the Tuskegee Institute show that in 1900, 106 black citizens were lynched in the United States (in comparison, 9 whites were lynched that year); in 1930, 20 black citizens were lynched (1 white was lynched that year); 24 black citizens were lynched in 1933, and 18 in 1935. In 1936, without the force of federal legislation compelling Washington to put an end to the horrific practice, the number of lynchings of black Americans fell to 8, and declined—if maddeningly slowly—in the decades that followed. Until 1938, out of its headquarters high above Fifth Avenue in Manhattan, the NAACP flew a black-and-white flag with a chilling reminder: A MAN WAS LYNCHED YESTERDAY.

Though he first resisted getting drawn into Walter White's public spectacles, preferring instead to focus on the plodding, deliberate campaign pioneered by Charles Houston to transform American society through the law, Marshall came to see the value in projecting soft power to transform the culture. He took on his own mini-crusade to get the American Tobacco Co.—the conglomerate formed in 1890 by J. B. Duke, whose fortune would one day undergird Duke University—to discontinue use of the tobacco brand name "Nigger Hair." During his cross-country travels for the NAACP, Marshall built on an earlier success in securing equal pay for black teachers in his home state of Maryland by meeting with black teachers and lawyers locally to encourage and help them to organize legal challenges to the race pay gap in their own states. Marshall joined in White's antilynching campaign, lobbying members of Congress in DC and tracking the progress—or lack thereof—of antilynching legislation.

Notwithstanding his forays into traditional activism, congressional lobbying, and the like, the bulk of Marshall's work remained in the legal office, where he stayed as busy as he could stand to be. A hectic travel itinerary kept him crisscrossing the country on buses and trains at a fevered pace, representing clients who had been wronged on account of their race and, perhaps of greater importance, whose cases might establish legal precedent that would reach far beyond any single client's plight and thus move the needle for black Americans in favor of full racial equality before the law. Though the passage of the Fourteenth Amendment in 1868 had enshrined full protection of the law to all citizens equally, day-to-day life for black Americans hardly reflected that promise. Little had been done to apply those protections at the state level, and virtually no progress would be made on that front until momentous Supreme Court decisions found that the promise of equal protection of law required the states to extend those protections to black Americans. This reality illustrates the hard-nosed truth that underpinned the NAACP's legal work:

the constitution of the United States means what the Supreme Court says it means. Under Charles Houston, the NAACP's legal program had embarked on a crusade that was both stealthy and extraordinarily ambitious; theirs would be a clandestine insurrection to transform America's oppressive and racist legal system from within.

Black citizens throughout the country, but particularly in the South, lived under a variety of racist legal codes and traditions, known commonly as Jim Crow laws, designed to systematically block African Americans from attaining any meaningful degree of economic, social, or political power. Black citizens throughout the South were barred from voting in elections or from taking part in the primaries through which the Democratic Party selected its candidates, effectively excluding them from the political process entirely in the Democratic Party–dominated South. Black teachers were paid less than white, black schools funded less per pupil than their white counterparts, and black students barred from attending most state universities and professional schools.

The entire edifice of this program of systemic black oppression rested on a legal doctrine of "separate but equal" that emerged from the 1896 Supreme Court case *Plessy v. Ferguson*, in which the court upheld the right of a railroad to remove Homer Plessy from a first-class car after he, in a highly orchestrated act of civil disobedience, informed the railroad that he was one-eighth black, sufficiently African in Louisiana for him to be barred from the whites-only section of the train. The decision upheld the legality of segregated facilities that were then cropping up across the South in the years after Reconstruction, when occupying Union troops pulled out and former Confederates sought to reassert white supremacy. This new regime of segregation used laws and mores to buttress white dominance and render black Americans politically impotent.

The separate but equal doctrine would allow public institutions to remain segregated so long as the state provided facilities for black citizens equal to those for whites. But the doctrine was a farce. The institutions that upheld white supremacy in the United States had no real interest in creating equal facilities for black Americans, and even if they had, such a proposition—creating two of everything—would have been prohibitively expensive. Many states lacked any professional schools for black students, and even in elementary schools where separate facilities did exist they were hardly equal. Thurgood Marshall's alma mater in Baltimore was the only high school in the city for black students, and it also served black students from surrounding counties. The severely overcrowded building lacked a cafeteria, auditorium, gymnasium, or any large meeting space—for any large gatherings the school had to borrow space from a nearby church or theater.

Faced with an entrenched system of racial apartheid backed by Supreme Court precedent, in 1930 the NAACP commissioned attorney Nathan Margold, a Romanian-born Jewish immigrant and recent Harvard Law graduate, to devise a strategy to combat the legal underpinnings of Jim Crow. The resulting Margold Report called for a surgical assault on segregation. Rather than attack separate but equal head on, the activist attorneys would instead use the doctrine to require that separate schools for black students be truly equal to schools for whites. The plan was to turn a mirror on American society, using the American legal tradition to reveal "separate but equal" for the absurdity that it was by showing not just that separate facilities for black Americans tended to be unequal, but that separate was inherently unequal.

As lead attorney for the NAACP, Charles Houston took the Margold Report battle plan a step further. Less than hopeful about his prospects for success in a full-frontal assault on segregation in public schools, Houston orchestrated a more subtle, long-term strategy to build new legal precedent against the separate but equal doctrine slowly and methodically starting with graduate schools. Though the strategy trained its crosshairs on segregation in the education system, the ultimate target was the very concept of second-class citizenship in the United States, a country in which the inequality of races had been written into its constitution. What Houston had in mind was nothing less than a revolution. The movement would reshape the law from within, establishing legal precedent case by case, like stonemasons laying brick, until they had built a body of case law that would force the system to over-throw itself. When he took the reins of the NAACP's legal depart-ment, Marshall became the lead commander in the operation.

One major challenge the lawyers faced in implementing their strategy emerged from the tradition in American law, and in English Common Law from which it descended, known as *locus standi*, or "standing." American courts exist not to right wrongs but to provide recourse when a person has been wronged—which is to say that a person must be able to show he or she has been harmed in order to seek recourse from the courts. Using the courts to change the law required finding actual people whom the law had harmed. What Marshall needed weren't merely clients opposed to segregation but people whose lives had been materially and adversely affected by Jim Crow in its various manifestations. The strategy thus depended on the cooperation of real people, in all their imperfect humanity, which occasionally caused the move-ment to hit a speed bump.

In *Gaines v. Canada*, Houston made an early dent in the sep-arate but equal doctrine when the Supreme Court ruled in 1938 that Missouri had to either let his black client study at the state's public law school or set up a law school especially for black stu-dents. Rather than admit Lloyd Gaines to the state's law school in the wake of the ruling, the state promised to build him his own school. But meanwhile, apparently buckling under the pressure of intense public attention on the high-profile case, Gaines became increasingly erratic. Eventually, he simply disappeared, forcing the attorneys to drop the matter. In 1940, Marshall tried again, this time filing to force the University of Missouri's journalism school to accept a black applicant. Rather than comply, Missouri simply shut down the school, illustrating the lengths to which segregationists would go to keep black citizens away from the sources of white power.

Often Marshall's travels throughout the American South landed him in real physical danger, as was the case when he traveled to Dallas to strike a blow against Texas's policy—in flagrant violation of the United States Supreme Court—of not allowing African Americans to serve on juries. In 1938, local junior college president Dr. George F. Porter appeared for jury duty and stunned local authorities when he refused to be dismissed from the jury pool because he was black, as was the custom. Two white men answered Porter's intransigence by grabbing him by the collar, walking him out of the building, and tossing him headfirst down the courthouse steps. Scraped and bruised, Porter got to his feet and forced his way past the two men and back into the building. He made it back to the courtroom, where the judge said his appeal had been noted but dismissed him again, this time ordering sheriff's deputies to escort him to safety.

According to Marshall biographer Juan Williams, when word got around that NAACP lawyer Thurgood Marshall intended to come to town to investigate the state's illegal policy of denying black citizens the right to serve on juries, the local chief of police ordered that his men not lay a hand on Marshall, because, he said, "I personally will take him and kick the shit out of him. Personally." On learning of the threat, Marshall asked for protection from the governor, who assigned a Texas Ranger as his

bodyguard. Once, after a day of meetings at the courthouse, the
protection came in handy when the police chief spotted Marshall
walking down the front steps and came charging at him, gun
drawn, shouting, "Hi, you black son of a bitch! I've got you now!"
The ranger, sitting on the hood of Marshall's car, drew his own
gun and ordered the raging cop to stand down.

Facing such threats to his personal safety, Marshall nevertheless
acted boldly and strategically in his travels throughout the South.
As he traveled by train from town to town—in an era before
the interstate highway system, when many roads in rural America, especially in the South, remained unpaved—Marshall would
meet with local chapters of the NAACP to update members on
goings-on at the national office, raise money, and spread a little
hope and good cheer amid the long battle for black liberation. He
dined high and low with gusto and gratitude all the same. "Back
then you could lose your job just for joining the NAACP," recalled
Mildred Byrd, the wife of former Harlem Globetrotter Daniel Byrd
who became Marshall's regular companion on nights out in New
Orleans for crawfish and booze. "All these little one-horse towns
we used to take him to. And those people didn't have much to
offer. We might have to sit at a table in the kitchen with a lamp-
light, and those people would be serving their little meager dishes
to us. He would just sit there and eat it like it tastes like turkey.
Thurgood, he was humble as a lamb. Because sometimes the gravy
looked black as my daughter's hair, but it tasted good and they
would just serve what they had." Marshall spent his nights in the
homes of black families, but for their safety and his own he rarely
stayed in the same house twice. And though his mere presence in
many southern towns was in itself an act of defiance, when the
situation called for it Marshall would "yes, sir" even the dumbest
redneck if it meant avoiding an unnecessary conflict that might
put him in jail—or the grave. The NAACP's mission to dethrone

Jim Crow from behind enemy lines was too important to allow distractions.

On the whole, by 1940 Marshall's work at the helm of the NAACP's legal department was building real momentum within the movement. Though Marshall did not ultimately take legal action against anyone in the Porter case, as a result of the national attention his office brought on the case a black man served in a jury in Dallas within weeks, and gradually the habits formed by the old policy simply dissipated. Dallas juries came to more accurately reflect the racial makeup of the city. After trying for more than a decade, the NAACP nearly scored another victory in Texas when—for the fourth time in fifteen years—it sued the state Democratic Party for excluding black citizens. Once he'd raised the money, found a client, and obtained a hearing in a Houston courtroom, Marshall was confident of a victory. The discovery at the last minute that his client had merely tried to vote in a runoff, not the primary itself, and thus did not have standing to sue, was a devastating blow for the local black community. The tireless Marshall would devote the next few years to raising yet more money, finding yet another plaintiff, and finally getting his day in court with the Texas Democratic Party.

But the case that the thirty-one-year-old attorney took in front of the nation's highest court on January 4, 1940, was his most high-stakes yet, and the first case Marshall argued as lead counsel before the US Supreme Court without the leadership of his mentor Charles Houston. When, on February 12, 1940, the high court handed down its decision on *Chambers v. Florida*, a criminal matter involving the robbery and murder of an elderly white man, Marshall, only seven years out of law school, won a stunning victory. The defendants' confessions were found to have been clearly coerced, though without violence, and therefore held to be inadmissible as evidence. It was Marshall's first solo win before the US Supreme Court. The young lawyer newly at the helm of the nation's preeminent African American civil rights organization was broke but brimming with confidence.

The impact of that win would reverberate far beyond Washington. It meant that Marshall's fundamental argument—that black Americans, including black criminal defendants, are equal citizens entitled to the protections provided to all citizens by the United States Constitution—had been accepted, in at least this instance, by the nation's highest court. With the NAACP desperate to build momentum for its ambitious plan to overturn Jim Crow, Marshall was in search of a client whose case would grab newspaper headlines and inspire outrage—like, for instance, a black man wrongly accused of an especially heinous murder. The *Chambers* case signaled that a black criminal defendant could also win in the high court.

The confluence of those revelations would change the course of American civil rights history. It would also change the life of a young man in a small town in southeastern Oklahoma who just weeks earlier had been arrested for the murder of the Rogers family.

2

NEWS OF THE Rogers family's grim fate arrived like an earth-quake in Choctaw County. In the darkness the evening before, the burning farmhouse could be seen from up to a mile away, and with rumors spreading fast between the small towns along the stretch of Highway 70 that ran from Hugo east through Sawyer, Fort Towson, Swink, and Idabel in the far southeastern corner of the state, authorities began investigating immediately. After James Glenn caught a ride on the highway the night of the murder, the boy and his baby brother had been taken to stay with their uncle, Vernon Colclasure, their mother's brother. That very night, a stunned and shaken James Glenn spoke to law enforcement, and soon the bare facts of the case painted for county attorney Norman Horton a clear if sparse picture of what had transpired.

On Tuesday, January 2, Choctaw County residents eager for news about the fire picked up the day's issue of the the *Hugo Daily News*, the county's biggest newspaper, to find a shocking single headline splashed in large font across the top of the page: "MURDER BEYOND DOUBT," SAYS HORTON. A subheadline below declared: "Frightened Boy Sticks to Story: 'Two Men Shot Papa, Mama.'"

The paper recounted the few facts then known about the grue-some tale, describing how the only living eyewitness old enough to speak to the police was dazed as he recounted the horrifying moment when his parents were brutally murdered. "They shot Papa through the window. Mama said, 'Oh, my' and ran out the back door. They shot her too," he said.

A report in a sidebar next to the paper's lead story captured the pandemonium that erupted on New Year's Eve after the murder. That night, another uncle of the surviving boys contacted the *Hugo Daily News* to notify the press of the tragedy. Soon after, the man was riding in a car with Deputy Sheriff Van Raulston and Roy Marshall, a Choctaw County barber. The three were driving to the scene of the fire when their vehicle collided with another car, driven, the paper reported, by a "Mississippi Negro." It would have been a chaotic scene: three men careening fast, frenzied, and recklessly in the darkness down a rural two-lane highway back toward the site of a grisly murder and a house still in flames, in the mayhem crashing into another vehicle on the road. The uncle was hospitalized for his injuries. "[Roy] Marshall's back was injured, and Raulston suffered a broken nose, cuts and bruises," the paper reported tersely. And toward the end of the article: "All six of the Negroes in the [other] car were also taken to Hugo Hospital."

In the days that followed, the investigation proceeded quickly. An x-ray of Elmer Rogers's remains revealed a torso full of buckshot, indicating a shotgun had been used in the crime. In the smoldering ruins of the immolated farmhouse, investigators found broken pieces of Marie Rogers's jaw, suggesting her face had been split by a heavy instrument, such as an ax. Both her and her husband's heads had apparently been crushed by similarly heavy blows. While sifting through the crime scene, Sheriff Roy Harmon and others discovered two sets of footprints in the snow leading away from the house and followed them due north and west, but lost the trail after a mile.

Law enforcement's first real break in the case came via a tip from the assistant warden at the prison near Stringtown, seventy miles northwest, which led to the arrest of Frank Wellmon, a convict serving time at a work camp near Sawyer, the town just six miles west along the highway from Fort Towson. A white man in his forties, Wellmon was nearly halfway through a thirty-year sentence for killing his wife. He'd been incarcerated at the Stringtown prison for a short time before being transferred to the work camp near Sawyer, where prisoners labored in the gravel pits to produce raw material for paving the highways.

Details are scant on what precisely the assistant warden told Choctaw County law enforcement, but press reports from the time indicate that Wellmon was acquainted in some way with Marie Rogers. Among people in Fort Towson and the surrounding towns, incendiary rumors began to spread of a dice game at the home of a disabled Native American woman named Conley: her home may have doubled as a brothel, some said; the scene was redolent with wildcat whiskey and greed; some said convicts from the nearby chain gang gambled there with a mixed-race group of local townspeople, Elmer Rogers among them. Some said Elmer won a killing that night, and that the men who'd lost their money to him murdered to get it back.

Perhaps due to the tip, perhaps spurred by rumors, by Tuesday, January 2, as another bout of freezing cold weather settled bitterly over southeastern Oklahoma, Sheriff Harmon had Frank Wellmon in custody for questioning. Wellmon denied any knowledge of the murders but, Harmon told a reporter, he "appeared nervous."

By late 1939, the prison work camp between Sawyer and Fort Towson had become a political time bomb. Security at the camp was known to be lax. Trustees—convicts allowed to live at lower security camps where they labored on public works projects, like the Fort Towson Dam and the highway gravel pit—roamed freely, coming and going as they pleased, especially on weekends. Some trustees dated women in Fort Towson or Sawyer. One fancied himself a preacher, holding weekly church services at a school-house. It was an open secret that prisoners drank whiskey at the camp, in violation of both camp regulations and state law in offi-cially dry Oklahoma. For many locals, having convicted criminals who were still serving time roaming freely in their towns had become more than a nuisance. The patience of local citizens was being pushed to its limits.

The official who oversaw the camp had been appointed by Jess Dunn, warden of the state prison at McAlester, who had been appointed by the governor himself. The locals' growing resentment of the casual atmosphere around the work camp ensured that even the smallest spark had the potential to ignite a political firestorm that in seconds would reach to the highest office in the state. The Rogers murder was a conflagration.

This may explain why the very day that news emerged of Wellmon's arrest and interrogation, the governor's recent appointee Warden Dunn visited the camp to conduct a "routine inspection" and was quoted in the newspaper saying he believed the wrong man had been arrested for the crime. "Willmon [*sic*] was in church Sunday night," he told a reporter. But county attorney Norman Horton still thought Wellmon was likely guilty. The suspect kept altering his story, changing the time of his return to the work camp on Sunday night, Horton said. And another rumor emerged that a Sawyer woman could provide an alibi for Wellmon, who, she said, was at her house on Sunday until midnight, or thereabouts, contradicting Dunn's insistence that the man had been at church all evening.

The story emerging in Choctaw County regarding convicts at a local prison camp and a horrific triple murder on New Year's Eve was beginning to have the makings of a serious political prob-lem for the governor. Leon "Red" Phillips—nicknamed owing to his bright red hair—had been elected in 1938 after an especially contentious race to succeed the state's New Deal–supporting governor. Though he professed tepid loyalty to President Roosevelt during the campaign, once elected Phillips began a ruthless assault on the New Deal programs coming out of Washington. An imposing figure who weighed nearly three hundred pounds and was rarely seen without a cigar sticking out the corner of his mouth, Phillips enjoyed a well-earned reputation for brutality in politics. One contemporary described him as "impulsive in action, belligerent by nature," and a "three-hundred pound giant [who] waded into conflict with the alacrity of a young pugilist" with "no capacity for tact in speech and diplomacy in action." The list of character traits later historians used to describe Phillips's personality is revealing enough on its own: sullen, humorless, vindictive, obstinate, and prone to all-consuming personal hatred.

On Thursday, January 4—the same day FDR nominated his attorney general Frank Murphy to sit on the US Supreme Court, while Germany barreled across Europe and another round of snow and sleet blanketed Choctaw County—the governor told the *Hugo Daily News* he was convinced of Wellmon's innocence. Governor Phillips personally dispatched a "special investigator" from his office to look into the matter.

By January 9 local officials had landed on a second suspect, a Sawyer man named Houston Lambert, and then a third, another trustee from the prison camp named Floyd Carpenter. News of the arrests made the papers on January 11 by way of a statement made to the sheriff by Lambert's aunt, a seventy-two-year-old woman named Pruda May Wortz. HUGO WOMAN MAY HAVE SOLUTION TO FORT TOWSON MURDER MYSTERY, read the headline in large print across the front page. In her statement, as printed in the *Daily News*, Wortz told officials she had come forward to exonerate her nephew.

The Wednesday after New Year's, she said, two younger women—Lambert's sister-in-law and another woman named Conley—came to her home and recounted how the night of the murder the two convicts forced Lambert at gunpoint to drive the car for the crime. When they returned hours later, Lambert's hair was singed nearly off on one side, and his arm and shirt had been burned. Back at the house, Wellmon close cropped Lambert's hair and had him wash his head twice, she said.

"Did you ever at any time, Grandma, have any trouble with Houston?" Sheriff Harmon asked.

"No Sir, never," she said. "He was always my favorite nephew and always a good boy."

"Then your only motive in coming to us with this statement is to help us get justice?"

"Yes. I want to protect him," she said. "I believe they was making a scapegoat out of him."

The next day, Houston Lambert offered a full confession with a reporter from the *Hugo Daily News* present. The paper reprinted his statement, heralding the news with a long, bold-faced headline: OFFICERS BREAK MURDER MYSTERY; TWO SAWYER CONVICTS IDENTIFIED.

> Houston Lambert of Sawyer changed his story about the slaying of the Rogers family late this morning and has admitted before the officers that he was present but did not participate in the slaying of the Rogers family or the burning of the house.
>
> Early this morning Lambert made a statement before representatives of the *Daily News* in which he outlined his actions and the fact that two men had forced him to take his mother-in-law's car and go with them to a point near the scene and await their return.

When faced by his mother-in-law and in the face of quizzing Lambert admitted that he did not take Mrs. Frank's car but early New Year's Eve night Wellman [*sic*], Carpenter and another convict whom they called "Doug" came to his home and asked him to walk down the road with them. During the conversation they told him that they were going to Rogers' home and rob him of $80 that it was claimed that Rogers won in a crap game the day before. En route they commandeered a car and drove it to the home of Rogers where he witnessed the slaying of Mr. Rogers and heard the shots and blows that killed Mrs. Rogers.

Explaining why his hair was singed he stated in his last statement that he heard the baby crying in the house and attempted to rescue it and was burned in his futile effort to rescue the child from the burning building. Lambert stated that the killing was done with a sawed off shotgun but he didn't say where the shotgun came from or where it was taken after the killing. It was known that there was a shotgun at the prison camp. He also states that the car Lambert claimed to have commandeered is said to have belonged to a convict at the Sawyer camp.

That same day, prison warden Jess Dunn announced that discipline would be tightened at the prison camp and the sergeant in charge replaced.

Lambert's full, detailed confession would seem to have been the beginning of the end for the investigation. But such was not the case. On January 14, the newspaper reported that Lambert had inexplicably changed his story yet again, this time adding the bizarre implication of a black man who heretofore had no connection to the investigation at all.

"Upon checking and rechecking," the paper reported, "it was found that the Negro, whose name is D. W. Jordan, who lives three and one-half miles south of Sawyer, could not drive a car, never owned a car and was the father of 13 children." Lambert's story continued to change over the course of several days. He implicated others, including his brother-in-law and sister-in-law. He told officials where he hid the gun and ax used in the murder, but extensive searches turned up neither weapon.

What went unreported in the local paper in the days after Lambert's first confession on January 12 was that on that very day another man had been arrested in connection with the investigation. He had been held and interrogated incommunicado, without the knowledge of the general public, all while Lambert's numerous confessions were followed closely and reported on in detail by the local press. The new suspect was poor and black, an occasional farmhand with a petty criminal record. Just twenty years old, he had already served one year in prison for burglary and nearly two years on a larceny conviction for stealing chickens. He had gone by a few names, including W.D. Gardner and W.D. Fleeks, but his true name, he said, was W.D. Lyons.

The citizens of Choctaw County had been following the sensational story closely in the local papers, and the investigation seemed to be adding up, in fits and starts, to an explanation that pointed to convicted criminals at a local prison camp where rules were known to be lax. Thus, it came as a shock to many when on Tuesday, January 23, they opened copies of the *Hugo Daily News* to find the most bizarre headline yet about the Fort Towson murder mystery: NEGRO ADMITS MURDER OF 3.

The article reported that at about 2:30 AM that Tuesday morning, just before the paper went to press, "after a cross-fire examination by officers," Lyons admitted to murdering the Rogers family. He also identified an accomplice, the paper said, named

Van Bizzell, who was subsequently arrested but who resolutely denied any knowledge of the crime. The paper noted that "Houston Lambert evidently has passed out of the picture as far as the murder is concerned. The officers applied the lie detector to him Monday afternoon and he said that he had nothing to do with the murder, knew nothing about it, and that the convict Thompson and Lois Rainey [whom he had implicated earlier] likewise had no part in the murder." The paper spent more than a little ink in an effort to explain why Lambert had been lying all this time about his own guilt. Noting that law enforcement wasted a lot of time and money chasing leads from Lambert's confessions, the paper stated that "when asked why all of these stories, he is alleged to have said that he began lying at the first and would tell another one to correct a statement he had made in a former statement and that he knew all the time that he was lying."

In a follow-up story the next day, the paper offered a detailed account of Lyons's supposed confession: He borrowed a shotgun from his friend Sammy Green and approached Van Bizzell with the idea of robbing Elmer Rogers. It was Bizzell who shot Mr. Rogers, then Mrs. Rogers, and who then mutilated her body with an ax. The two ransacked the house, stole $4.15 off Mr. Rogers's corpse, poured coal oil throughout the structure, set it on fire, and escaped. Lyons had been arrested, the paper reported with telling ambiguity, "following a tip that he might be connected with the crime." Authorities later picked up "several clues"—none identified in the paper—that pointed to Lyons.

W.D. Lyons and Van Bizzell were each charged with three counts of murder, one count of arson, and one count of robbery with a firearm. The two were arraigned together on Saturday, January 27, following a day of testimony from law enforcement and witnesses with circumstantial evidence, like the fact that Lyons was

seen carrying a gun the day of the murder. Bizzell was represented
by an attorney, but Lyons had no counsel.

Many in Choctaw County did not believe the story. Everyone
knew rules at the prison camp often went unenforced and that
convicted criminals came and went from the camp at their leisure.
Newspaper readers had closely followed developments after the
murder, as Houston Lambert's story began to come together piece
by piece, with corroborating witnesses. Astute political observers
knew that if a scandal erupted connecting the poorly run prison
camp to a macabre triple murder, all local politicians would be
on the hook for it in upcoming elections, and that, having barely
eked out a victory in the 1938 Democratic gubernatorial primary
(for all practical purposes the general election in Oklahoma at
the time), Governor Phillips would also be weakened by any such
scandal. Cynical observers might have seen hints of invisible forces
at work behind the scenes attempting to influence the investigation, perhaps to get Lambert to twist his story to their own
purposes, as the tale changed from day to day spontaneously and
seemingly arbitrarily, first naming one accomplice, then another,
for a moment implicating a black man named D.W. before authorities got a confession out of another named W.D.

Fort Towson resident Myrtle Collins, a white woman, recalled
years later that many in town did not believe Lyons was guilty,
and that even at the time many figured the only piece of real evidence other than his confession that seemed to connect Lyons to
the crime, a child's recollection of seeing a black hand during the
attack, was most easily accounted for by the simplest explanation:
it was dark and on that cold, snowy night the intruders wore
gloves. Charles Collins, Myrtle's brother, whose father worked as
a guard at the prison camp, recalled his father and others talking
openly on the porch of his home about how the lawmen were

railroading Lyons, trying to pin the crime on an innocent man while setting the guilty parties free.

But this was still Little Dixie, still the rural American South in the clutches of Jim Crow, decades before federal civil rights protections for black Americans seemed a realistic possibility, a time when an idea as far-fetched as integrated public schools in Oklahoma belonged more to the realm of science fiction than contemporary reality. There had not yet been a Malcolm X or a March on Washington for Jobs and Freedom—three days after Lyons was arrested, Martin Luther King Jr. celebrated his eleventh birthday.

Amid the confusion of rumors, conflicting newspaper reports, and official statements from the authorities, who still had the trust of the community they served, it was, perhaps, easy enough to believe that Lyons and Bizzell might have murdered the Rogers family. One of the men had confessed, after all. And the little boy had seen a black hand. As often happened in the South when news of this sort hit the papers, racial tensions began to simmer. The atmosphere was tense in Little Dixie when the men appeared in court to be arraigned on their charges Saturday, January 27, 1940. In its Sunday edition the next day, the *Hugo Daily News* reported, "The court house lawn and building took on a military air early Saturday morning" as nearly forty national guardsmen were deployed to Hugo to maintain order and safeguard the court proceedings.

On the other hand, a close read of the newspaper, which seems at pains to justify the actions of local officials, might suggest that the National Guard had been called out for other purposes—that fears of unrest may have had less to do with black men accused of murder than with local law enforcement arresting innocent men while letting the guilty men go free. "For the past week tension has been very high in some circles," the paper said, "and a feeling has been intense against the two Negroes that were being held, one of whom had confessed to the murder of the Rogers family on New Year's Eve night. The governor's decision to call out the National Guard as a precaution against violence, has been praised by those in close contact with the situation."

3

VAN BIZZELL FOUND an attorney soon after his arrest, and seven months later, on July 10, 1940, he was released on bond. According to newspaper accounts, he was told to leave Choctaw County and never return.

For a year after his arrest, W.D. Lyons languished in jail awaiting trial. This fact in itself speaks volumes. For a black man accused of robbing and brutally murdering a white man, woman, and child in southeastern Oklahoma to sit in jail without trial for months would have been extremely odd in 1940—waiting a year was simply unheard of. Two decades earlier, in the comparatively cosmopolitan city of Tulsa, a white woman falsely accused a black man of groping her in the elevator of a commercial building downtown; it wasn't a full twenty-four hours before the incident sparked one of the worst outbursts of mob violence in American history, unleashing two horror-filled days of arson and brutality that thoroughly decimated twenty-five square blocks of Greenwood, a section of town also known as Black Wall Street. The violence claimed untold numbers of lives—the Red Cross estimated three hundred dead, nearly all of them black, though some estimates put the death toll much higher. Though twenty years had passed since the Tulsa massacre and much had changed, much also remained the same. Even if by 1940 Lyons was less likely to be summarily sprung out of jail and lynched, the white political establishment would almost certainly have moved swiftly and decisively to see him convicted and executed had there been a general confidence in the guilt of the suspect. But it didn't, because there wasn't.

Mere days after Lyons's arrest, whispers began to emerge that interrogation techniques more severe than "cross-fire examination" were used to get a confession out of him. After a time, Lyons's wife and sisters had been allowed to see him; they saw his blackened eye, bruised back and arms, and the way he needed to lean on them in order to hobble around in his cell, unable to stand on his own. Lyons declined to tell them he was being beaten—perhaps he wanted to avoid worrying them any more than necessary, or he had been threatened with even worse treatment if he talked about his ordeal—but they could draw their own conclusions from his condition.

And there was more. White citizens heard law enforcement talk openly about beating a confession out of him. One man in particular, Vernon Cheatwood, the special investigator sent by Governor Phillips himself to take part in the investigation, boasted in the public lobby of the Webb Hotel in Hugo, where he was lodging, of using what he called his "nigger beater"—a leather strap with a pouch on one end loaded with buckshot, also called a black-jack—to beat a confession out of the young suspect. Cheatwood also bragged of it and showed off the weapon to the murdered woman's own father and sister-in-law. As the rumor mill churned, whispers spread of a pan of human bones employed in some way during the brutal interrogation that extracted a confession out of W.D. Lyons.

Roscoe Dunjee was born in 1883 in Harpers Ferry, West Virginia. Dunjee's father, the son, according to family lore, of John Tyler, the tenth president of the United States, was enslaved in Virginia and escaped through the Underground Railroad to Canada before returning to the United States to become a Baptist minister and found a local newspaper, the *Harpers Ferry Messenger*. He also helped start or operate a handful of colleges for black students. In 1892, the elder Dunjee was sent by the American Baptist Home Missionary Society to spread the gospel in the Oklahoma Territory, where the stern patriarch and his wife raised Roscoe and his four siblings at first in a dugout hovel in Choctaw (the oldest chartered town in the territory). In time the family moved into a more suitable house, where Dunjee encouraged his children to read from his considerable library, though he forbade novels in his home. Young Roscoe thus educated himself in his father's extensive, if prudish, book collection. At age fifteen, he became a member of the first class at Langston University, Oklahoma's proud new college open to black students, where he worked as a newspaperman for the local *Langston City Herald*.

After his father died in 1903, Roscoe Dunjee supported his mother and siblings by growing vegetables and selling them from a cart in towns near the family farm. Occasionally, the largely self-taught avid reader wrote articles for a newspaper owned by a friend, and by 1914 he scraped together enough money to buy a small, old printing press of his own. On the humble foundation of that investment, Dunjee raised the *Black Dispatch*.

In the decades after the Civil War, African American newspapers were founded to cater to the black population moving en masse off the plantations and sharecropping farms to the cities. The *Black Dispatch* was one such paper, headquartered in Oklahoma City, though it became an important voice in the African American press nationwide. As its publisher—and head of the NAACP in Oklahoma—Dunjee had what most black Americans at the time did not: a voice in the public square and influence in the still nascent civil rights movement. Dunjee broadcast the audacity and boldness of his vision for the newspaper right from the start; reappropriating racist slang, the paper took its name from an old expression for unreliable rumor: "black dispatch gossip." "All of this has developed a psychology among Negroes that their color is a curse and that there is something evil in their peculiar pigmentation," Dunjee said when explaining the name years later. "It is my contention that Negroes should be proud to say, 'I am a black man.'"

The paper covered topics of special interest to its black readership—goings-on at Langston University and various African American fraternal organizations; news of racial unrest in other cities around the country; the publication of new books on subjects of interest to black readers, like the Underground Railroad; the opening of new theater productions with "all-star colored" casts—but it also served as a community forum like any local publication of its era. The paper carried mundane dispatches from communities around the country ("We are blessed to have beautiful sunny days nearly all this week" read one such tiny report from Gallup, New Mexico), scuttlebutt from Hollywood, divinations from Astrola the Psycho-mentalist in response to anonymous queries about the future, plus job listings and ads for toothpaste, cold medicine, hair dye, real estate, and the like.

Dunjee was among the first black leaders in Oklahoma to get news of Lyons's arrest. In his February 3, 1940, issue of the *Black Dispatch*, Dunjee ran a small item in the corner of a crowded front page with the headline, NEGRO HELD IN FT. TOWSON SLAYINGS AFTER WHITE MAN MAKES CONFESSION TO CRIME. In the sub-headline, Dunjee made reference to the rumors then circulating in Choctaw County—"Many Citizens Believe That Black Man Has Been Terrorized into Making Statement."

In the uncertain days immediately after Lyons's confession, when Dunjee feared that a white mob might make an attempt at vigilante justice, he felt he needed to find a white lawyer to represent the young man. Black attorneys were rare in Oklahoma in 1940, and none had ever appeared before a court in Choctaw County. He feared that hiring a black lawyer to represent Lyons in Little Dixie, a region known for its Confederate legacy, would stir up even more trouble. Making matters more difficult, representing the defendant in a case the governor had a personal interest in was, to understate Dunjee's predicament, an unpopular cause. Dunjee turned to a man who had the reputation for courage necessary to take the case, and who had made a career representing clients others wouldn't come near: Stanley Belden, a crusading Oklahoma lawyer with an unshakeable indignation at injustice.

Stanley Belden was born on March 15, 1898. He and eleven siblings were raised by poor sharecroppers who moved often from one farm to the next in Kansas and Oklahoma. When Belden was in the sixth grade his father was injured in a fall, and young Stanley was forced to leave school to help support the family by working on the farm.

Belden's parents were mainstream Protestant Christians, but his mother had grown up a Quaker. Perhaps it was this influence that led to his life of principled liberalism and independence of thought. One of his favorite poems was "Invictus" by the English poet William Ernest Henley. He committed it to memory and liked to recite its bracing lines aloud: "It matters not how strait the gate / How charged with punishments the scroll / I am the master of my fate / I am the captain of my soul."

During the First World War, Belden, at seventeen already a member of the Socialist Party of America, refused to be drafted to fight in a war he saw as senseless and immoral. He hid out during the war, and when it was over turned himself in to the authorities. At his trial, Belden declared, "I am proud to be a martyr." He spent ten months in a jail as a result.

While Belden was imprisoned, erstwhile Socialist Party presidential nominee and fellow conscientious objector Eugene V. Debs wrote to him, "In good time all will come right and you will stand forth and be vindicated." The judge who sentenced Belden was so impressed with him that he offered to pay if Belden would go to law school. Belden declined the offer, unwilling to depend on charity, but he took the inspiration. After serving his sentence he moved to Tennessee and enrolled in Cumberland University's two-year law program. He finished in a year.

Belden became Oklahoma's representative for the American Civil Liberties Union, and he made a career representing clients on the margins of Oklahoma society, including dispossessed Native Americans, religious minorities, socialists, and communists. When Belden was representing members of the Jehovah's Witnesses sect, who refused on religious grounds to pledge allegiance to the American flag, an Oklahoma judge ordered Belden to prove his loyalty by kissing the flag himself. Belden refused on principle, so the judge jailed him. By the time he was released a lynch mob had amassed outside the jail, and Belden demanded to remain behind bars until he could be guaranteed safe passage. Regarding another trial involving Jehovah's Witnesses, Belden wrote to the ACLU that a police officer warned him his "every move was being watched and that if I got outside of my county (where I was known) that my life was in danger." By the time Dunjee hired him to represent W.D. Lyons, Belden already had pariah status among Oklahoma's political elite.

For all his outsider status as a renegade lawyer, Belden did meet Dunjee's main criteria: he was competent, willing, and white, and thus able to operate in Choctaw County more or less freely in relative safety. Not long after Lyons's arrest in January 1940, Belden traveled to Hugo to visit the defendant and meet with others in town, black and white. During those meetings he learned more about Lyons's arrest and torture. He also found white citizens who said Cheatwood had admitted to them, proudly, that he had beaten a confession out of the young man.

Belden reported his findings back to Dunjee, who became more certain than ever not only that Lyons was innocent and that his arrest and torture had been a gross miscarriage of justice but also that this case was a winner in the courts of both law and public opinion. After Belden's initial investigation, Dunjee contacted his friend Thurgood Marshall at the national NAACP office to inform him of the developing situation.

During the year after Lyons was arrested, public sentiment, it seemed, had changed in Choctaw County. Eventually it became clear that blacks and whites alike were against local authorities; locals knew white convicts who were almost certainly guilty of the crime had been set free, and the political establishment had conspired to beat a confession out of the black man. In the 1940 local elections, months after Lyons's arrest, Sheriff Harmon was thrown out of office by a majority in his outraged community. As the new year—and the anniversary of the murder—approached, Marshall wrote to Belden directly to ask him for an overview of Lyons's predicament. On January 7, 1941, Belden wrote back.

> Dear Sir :
> In answer to your letter of December 30, 1940, I wish to state that I was in Hugo yesterday and W.D. Lyons' case is set for January 27, 1941.

I think this case is of great importance to your organization. This boy was beaten by the governor's special
investigator (according to the investigator's own statement
made before good, substantial citizens) for 6 solid hours
with a black-jack, "from his head to his feet—every inch
of his body" and by such means obtained a confession.

Lyons tells me that he did not commit the murder, but
finally said so in order to stop the punishment. Of course,
a confession, to be used in this state, must be free and
voluntary and I have the statement of one of the officers
made at the preliminary hearing that he saw some slapping
of the defendant by the officers.

A white boy was first arrested and charged with the
killing, and he confessed in detail to the murder; but later
repudiated his confession and told me that he confessed to
it because of the beating that he was given by the officers.

I expect to use the father, father-in-law, and grandfather
of the murdered family as to the special investigator's
boasting in his presence of having beat Lyons for hours
to get a confession.

I am of the opinion that because this case involves
the governor's office through his special investigator, a
great deal of pressure will be brought to bear from certain
sources.

We will be glad to have any assistance that you can
render us.

Very truly yours,
Stanley D. Belden

After receiving the letter, Marshall wrote immediately to Dunjee for clarification—had Belden's services been retained by the

NAACP? He wanted to make certain that the NAACP would be in charge—and in the headlines—as the case moved forward.

Dunjee responded on January 13:

> The Lyons case is set for trial January 27th, Hugo, Oklahoma. In answer to your question asked in today's letter, the case is an NAACP case. Stanley Belden is employed by our State Conference and was paid the $75.00 received from your office.
>
> Just as you think, I am of the opinion that this is one of the most important cases we have attacked. It is a perfect natural so far as winning it is concerned. The truth is that the Governor's office is going to turn heaven and earth to prevent witnesses appearing and a general campaign of intimidation has carried on in this way. This is the only way that the state can fight, for the facts and the evidence are all against the prosecution.

Dunjee suggested Marshall come down personally for the trial and to attend a few regional meetings to speak and raise money. "I believe you would be doing a fine thing to step in right at this point," he wrote,

> so that the National Office can take the spot-light and therefore revive association activity all over the U.S.
>
> I talked with Belden this morning and told him I was going to ask you to come down. He is deeply interested in the case but not entirely as aggressive as I would wish. He represents the American Civil Liberties Union in Oklahoma, and was one of the legal staff representing defendants in the Criminal Syndicalism trials here and he also has charge of cases for the Jehovah's Witnesses.

I employed Belden at a time when only a white man could have gone into Hugo, and at the request of Negroes in that section who advised me that relations between the races were very strained. It is well that I did employ Belden for he has been able to secure the testimony of a large number of whites who otherwise perhaps might have failed to testify.

As the matter stands now there is no ill feeling against Lyons. The community will be with him. Public sentiment has completely changed in and around Hugo. The only trouble will come from the officers who worked with the Governor's investigator. They are no longer officers, for the white and Negro citizens defeated the sheriff who served at the time Lyons was beaten.

I sent today for all of the January editions of the Paris, Texas, news as this paper carried the confession of the white man named Lambert, who confessed at first and told in detail how he committed the crime. It was only when the Governor discovered that convicts from a prison camp were implicated, and felt his administration might be scarred, that a black man was beaten into a confession.

Now I want you to understand that I really want you to come. I can arrange for the boys to hold at least two of their regional meetings while you are here and I am sure that your presence in the court room and other valuable assistance will mean much to the trial.

Thurgood Marshall responded with a short telegram, telling Dunjee that he'd like to help but money that January was especially tight. He wouldn't be able to make it to Oklahoma to assist with the murder case unless the Oklahoma office could advance him money for travel expenses. The national office would repay at least half, Marshall assured him, but they couldn't afford to cover costs up front.

At his office in Oklahoma City, Dunjee received an envelope stamped AIR MAIL and dated January 18, 1941, from the national NAACP office in New York. Dunjee might have guessed what the letter inside concerned, and considering the telegram he'd received he feared he knew the answer it contained.

"We simply do not have the money," Marshall wrote. He couldn't come. Alluding to his breakout victory in the *Chambers* case, Marshall wrote that "we all believe that this is a most important case and a sure winner under the recent U.S. Supreme Court decisions." But facts are stubborn things, particularly in accounting books, and the money simply was not there. A Connecticut rape case to which he was already committed (and which was much closer to the national office in New York than Oklahoma, which was three days from New York by train) would cost $600 more in court fees and expert witness payments. Payday for employees at the national office the week before had left the coffers almost completely empty. Marshall assured Dunjee that if Belden would mail him a letter laying out the facts of the case he would prepare a brief to submit to the court on behalf of the NAACP, but taking part himself was financially impossible.

After months advocating on Lyons's behalf, paying out of meager coffers for an attorney to represent him, and lobbying Marshall to come to Oklahoma to help with the case and raise much needed funds at a few local speaking engagements, Dunjee must have shared the exhausted frustration Marshall expressed in the letter's closing lines: "One of these days Negroes will support this organization in sufficient numbers and with sufficient money for us to do a real job. In the meantime, we will have to do the best we can."

But Dunjee wasn't done yet. As much as he disliked asking favors of anyone, as president of the Oklahoma NAACP Conference of

Branches he had grown accustomed to asking big favors of people with deep pockets. He knew one man in Oklahoma City whose pockets, he later wrote, were bulging with dough.

Dr. W. H. Slaughter was a wealthy physician and a longtime resident of Oklahoma City transplanted from Alabama. He owned rural land as well as properties inside the city, including the Slaughter Building, the commercial and social center of Oklahoma City's black neighborhood, the Deep Deuce. In the Slaughter Building, doctors and dentists kept offices by day, a young Ralph Ellison served soft drinks and ice cream as a soda jerk, and by night local jazz musicians wailed in the yellow lights of the rooftop garden. Slaughter's properties, the Slaughter Building most of all, had made him a very rich man. Dunjee needed cash fast, and Slaughter obliged with a ninety-dollar loan.

For Dunjee, taking a loan out to finance Marshall's trip to Oklahoma was a solid investment. He knew he could raise money by arranging speaking engagements for the young lawyer whose name was gaining serious currency in black communities as the man to turn to in a civil rights fight. And Dunjee, ever the newspaperman, saw the national story tucked away in a jail cell in southeastern Oklahoma.

He'd heard about Lyons's torture, the pan of bones, a family murdered and a child burned alive. The whole yarn had the makings of a sensational national story—the kind that sells newspapers—and national press meant national money. Dunjee hoped if he could get Marshall to Oklahoma and pique the interest of readers and other editors through his own newspaper, he might turn the story into a national event and rally blacks across the country to the poorly funded NAACP. He wrote to Marshall, telling him he'd already arranged for the muckraking magazine *Collier's Weekly* to run a story on the trial and imploring him not to miss this chance to do justice for a young man falsely accused and, not incidentally, to finally start raising much needed money. "You can see the importance of being in on the ground floor in this case," he wrote. "The Hugo community is for Lyons, it is only the Governor's office and a few petty officials who oppose Lyons' freedom."

Money at the NAACP was tight. Operating overhead for essentials like office stationary and train tickets for Marshall's frenetic travel representing clients across the country put manifest holes in the organization's coffers. All unspent expense money had to be returned to the office, and regular salary payments to the meager staff often left the group broke. Part of the problem stemmed from the fact that because the NAACP lobbied Congress—mainly in the frustratingly unsuccessful effort to secure passage of federal antilynching legislation—a donor could not write off donations to the group on his taxes. To get around that obstacle, on March 20, 1940, the NAACP turned Marshall's legal office into the NAACP Legal Defense Fund, ostensibly a separately funded and independent office within the NAACP, thus making donations to the fund tax deductible.*

The strategy was sensible, but it also put the LDF in an extremely precarious position, especially at the beginning. The distinction between the two entities was largely, in the words of Marshall biographer Juan Williams, "a sham," and at any moment the IRS might decide to have a closer look at the nonprofit group's

---

* In later years, facing intense scrutiny and intimidation from the Internal Revenue Service, the Legal Defense Fund would be spun off into a completely independent organization, so independent, in fact, that the two groups came into conflict decades later, culminating when the NAACP unsuccessfully sued the LDF for trademark infringement. At its inception with Marshall at the helm, however, the LDF was merely a financially independent unit within the civil rights group.

finances. Unable to legally draw resources from the NAACP, the less well-known LDF would then truly become entirely dependent on donations of its own. And in any case, neither the LDF nor the NAACP itself were fundraising powerhouses in 1940. Even the high-profile cases Marshall won, such as the desegregations suits against the University of Missouri and the University of Maryland law school, barely brought in enough donations to cover the costs of trying the cases themselves. The LDF was at every moment at death's door, barely able to keep the lights on week to week. Marshall desperately needed a case not only that he could win but also that in its ability to inspire shock and outrage would provide fodder for big-print newspaper headlines across the country—a case like the story of a vicious ax murder, a baby burned alive, a political scandal, murderers set free, an innocent man tortured with a blackjack and a pan of charred bones fighting for his life.

The day after he received the letter, Marshall wrote to Dunjee promising to come.

4

As THE BUS trundled southeast from Oklahoma City, it bumped
and jerked on the pitted highway, jostling passengers with
extra ferocity where Thurgood Marshall sat, in the back. Marshall's
always hectic travel schedule had been especially exhausting over
the past several days. Less than a week earlier, he'd been in Connecticut wrapping up the high-profile case of a black man accused
of raping a white woman. On Friday, he finished work on the case
and returned to New York just long enough for a bath and a change
of clothes before heading to the railroad station and boarding a
train bound for Oklahoma, arriving in Oklahoma City just after
8:00 AM Sunday morning. Dunjee was delighted and relieved to
see Marshall's tall and road-weary frame step out onto the train
station platform—the last he'd heard from the national office had
been a telegram informing him that Marshall had been held up by
developments in the Connecticut case, delaying his departure for
Oklahoma. After a quick pit stop at Dunjee's home, Marshall was
back on the road with his suitcase and a bag of peanuts, boiled
eggs, and bologna sandwiches—no telling where he'd be allowed to
order a meal on his journey into the heart of Little Dixie—riding in
the back of a bus bound for Hugo, where a young man he'd never
met was counting on him to save his life.

As the bus rolled down the road away from Oklahoma City,
the windswept flat expanses of the central Oklahoma plains gave

way to rolling hills and gray thickets of brittle trees, naked and hibernating for the winter. Then the hills became taller, the valleys deeper, and the gray leafless trees in winter streaming by in the frame of the bus window became streaked with green, as conifers entered the landscape. Finally, the bus descended out of the hills.

The bus depot glowed yellow under the streetlights when Marshall's bus came to a stop in Hugo nearly an hour after sunset. Marshall had heard about the National Guard being deployed to keep the peace during the preliminary hearing a year earlier, and he wasn't sure what reception to expect when he arrived. He climbed warily down the bus steps into the icy nighttime air, his breath condensing into puffs before him. Two men approached him in the darkness. They had never seen Marshall in person before, but a tall black man in a suit alighting a bus from Oklahoma City on a cold January night in 1941 in southeastern Oklahoma was not an especially common occurrence. They knew who he was.

One introduced himself as Dr. H. W. Williamston, a regional NAACP director and close friend to Roscoe Dunjee. The other, a white man, tall and thin like Marshall, was Stanley Belden. The two attorneys shook hands and exchanged pleasantries under the streetlights before hustling off to get down to business.

As they drove that night between Fort Towson, Sawyer, and Hugo to meet with as many locals as they could, Belden caught Marshall up on the details of the case. They discussed strategy and determined that Belden would lead the work of questioning and cross-examining witnesses while the prosecution presented its case. Belden had been on the case for the better part of a year, and his familiarity with the small details made him better poised to strike on any minor discrepancies and cracks in the prosecution's story. A good criminal defense attorney can chip away to turn those cracks into a fissure that might bring the entire case crumbling down. Marshall would lead when the defense presented its case and called its own witnesses, under the theory that the white men responsible for beating Lyons were unaccustomed to being forced to answer to a black man. They hoped that if Marshall pressed hard enough, and was insolent enough, the white lawmen might snap and lash out.

After their evening of preparation, Marshall went to the home of a local black resident who had volunteered to put him up for the night and tucked himself into bed. He needed the rest. W.D. Lyons's trial was set to begin the next morning.

In the street, horses tossed their tails over piles of manure that steamed in the cold January morning. A steady murmur rumbled over the grounds of the Hugo county courthouse that were swarming with people who had come from the surrounding areas in all modes of transportation—cars, trucks, horses, wagons, and some on the dinky, the short train that ran several times daily connecting Hugo with communities to the east, including Fort Towson, and as far as Idabel, fifty miles away. Most came simply to be a part of the excitement. They filled the courthouse halls and poured out onto the wide marble staircase. Women wore pressed church dresses and colorful hats festooned with feathers that bobbed up and down in the throng. Men wore suits, or pressed shirts tucked into khakis, or overalls and work boots caked in dirt fresh off the farm. A thousand or more people shuffled in the swarm around the courthouse, all here to witness a trial unlike any before in Choctaw County. As Marshall reported in a letter to his colleagues back in New York, word went around that "a nigger lawyer from New York" would represent the defendant, a young black man accused of a ghastly, atrocious crime. As far as anyone knew no black lawyer had ever appeared in court in Choctaw County, or anywhere in Little Dixie.

At 8:00 that morning Marshall and Belden met with their client. It was the first time Marshall and Lyons had met. Though they weren't able to speak for long Marshall sized up his new client and could see the man was telling the truth. If he wasn't already convinced of Lyons's innocence, after the meeting Marshall was sure of it.

The two lawyers walked into a courtroom jammed with people there to witness the spectacle. The din of chatter filled the room and a fog of cigar and cigarette smoke hung over the crowd. At the judge's bench on a raised platform several feet above the rest of the room, Judge George R. Childers took a seat in his black robe, puffing a fat cigar clinched between his teeth. He called the room to order and addressed some unfinished court business—several local officials, including the chief of police, had just been jailed for conspiring to sell illegal bootleg whiskey.

Judge Childers then called the Lyons case, and the attorneys walked up the aisle and took seats at their respective tables—on one side county prosecutor Norman Horton and deputy attorney general Sam Lattimore, who had been sent by Governor Phillips to assist with the case; on the other Stanley Belden and Thurgood Marshall. A bailiff led Lyons into the courtroom, where he sat in a chair next to his attorneys.

Before the start of official proceedings, Judge Childers addressed the overflow crowd in the gallery, with whites seated on one side and blacks on the other. "This is a trial between two nationalities," he said. He acknowledged that tensions ran high and public interest in the case was intense, and he cautioned that proper decorum be strictly enforced in his courtroom.

The first item of business the court addressed was to note for the record that codefendant Van Bizzell would be tried separately, an odd concession in the trial of black men accused of a heinous murder.

The trial began with the selection of a jury. All prospective jurors denied in no uncertain terms that they had any prejudice against black people. But each side in the case had objections. Some jurors were opposed to capital punishment, reason enough for the state to excuse them from duty. Some admitted they'd formed firmly held opinions about the murder—unsurprisingly, since both the arrest of convicts from the prison camp and W.D. Lyons's confession had been the subject of newspaper headlines and impassioned conversations in Choctaw County for more than a year. When the jury pool was exhausted the judge suggested the county attorney leave the courthouse to find more potential jurors. Marshall, Belden, and Dunjee—who had arrived late that morning and joined the others at the defense table—decided it best to go forward with what they had, lest Horton "go out and get his friends, relatives, etc.," Marshall later wrote. They withdrew their objections, and twelve jurors—all white men—were sworn to consider all the evidence presented in a fair and impartial manner and render a unanimous verdict.

Norman Horton, prosecuting attorney for Choctaw County, stood and presented his opening statement, intended to summarize the state's case against Lyons.

"Gentlemen of the jury," he said, looking toward the twelve white men seated in two rows in the jury box along the wall, "the Information in this case reads as follows."

Horton described for the jury how W.D. Lyons and an accomplice, Van Bizzell, snuck up to the Rogers home late at night on New Year's Eve, drunk on moonshine and driven by greed. He described how Lyons borrowed a shotgun from a friend and bought shotgun shells from the general store; how Lyons quietly approached the bedroom window, waited until Elmer Rogers was in sight, raised a single-barrel shotgun, and fired, shattering the glass and blasting buckshot into Elmer's ribs. How he then walked around the side of the house and shot Marie Rogers, hacked at her body with a double-bladed ax, and did the same to her husband. He described how Lyons set fire to the Rogers home with a child still inside, and that after the murder he ran to his grandmother's house, where he hid the gun. And he told the jury how, after days of interrogation, Lyons signed a confession, and later, in a "casual conversation" with a prison official, admitted, "me and Van Bizzell killed them people."

"And further, on making that proof we will ask you to send this defendant to the electric chair," he said, "where we feel that the perpetrator of such a hideous and diabolical crime should end his life." He waited a moment while the abhorrence of the crime and the gravity of the penalty of death hung in the air and sank into the minds of the jurors. "Thank you," he said finally, and sat down.

"Does the defense desire to reserve their statement?" Judge Childers asked Belden, seated next to his client at the defense table.

"The defendant desires to reserve their statement at this time," Belden said, thus concealing their defense strategy from the prosecution.

Marshall and Belden had agreed between themselves not to reveal their hand at the outset and instead let the prosecution make its case, with Belden making objections where appropriate to establish a record that poked holes in the prosecution's argument and lay the groundwork for an appeal should they lose in county court—"jury is lousy," Marshall later wrote in a letter to the national office. With Belden leading the first part of the trial, Marshall was freed up to focus on preparing what they knew would have to be the crux of their defense: suppressing the two confessions, one made twelve days after Lyons was first arrested and another made hours later at the prison in McAlester, by proving that both had been coerced through threats, sleep deprivation, and beatings.

"Call the State's first witness," Judge Childers said.

A timid child entered the gallery and walked up the aisle to the witness stand. The bailiff bent over to reach down with a Bible in hand. The little boy placed his hand on the book.

"Do you swear to tell the truth, the whole truth, and nothing but the truth, so help you God?" said the bailiff.

"Yes sir," said the boy.

As the child climbed into a seat on the witness stand, Judge Childers addressed the court reporter seated below and beside him. "Let the record show that Vernon Cheatwood, a State officer and an investigator out of the State office is excused from the rule," Childers said. "The rule" refers to the principle in American law that witnesses cannot be in the courtroom to hear other witnesses testify, unless allowed to be by the judge.

Belden looked quizzically at Childers. "Did you say he is excused from the rule?"

Belden knew that Cheatwood had been the ringleader in torturing Lyons—indeed, that he had in all likelihood orchestrated the entire travesty on behalf of Governor Phillips, setting the real murderers free and rounding up two black men to take the blame. Getting white citizens to testify to hearing Cheatwood brag about beating Lyons, a central piece of their defense, would be much harder if the hard-nosed governor's man with a reputation for brutality was staring up at witnesses from the gallery. Cheatwood's testimony, in which they hoped to trip him up, was similarly important for the defense they intended to present. Allowing him to watch the trial unfold, hearing the evidence presented leading up to his own testimony, could imperil their entire case.

"Yes, he is excused," Childers said, "being a State officer, and the investigator out of the Governor's office."

"We would like an exception to that," Belden said, putting his first objection into the court record before the first witness had even testified.

"Show their exception," Childers ordered the court reporter.

County attorney Norman Horton stood before the little boy on the witness stand. "Your name is James Glenn Rogers?" Horton said gently.

"Yes sir."

"How old are you, Glenn?"

"Eight."

"Eight years old," Horton said. "Where do you live now?"

"Berwyn," the boy said, a tiny town in nearby Carter County where he was staying with relatives.

"Did you ever live down here in Choctaw County, close to Fort Towson?"

"No." The child was shaken and confused.

Horton tried to redirect the question. "Do you remember when your mother and father got killed?"

"Last year," Glenn said.

"Do you know where you were living then? When they were killed?"

"Fort Towson."

"Fort Towson? Were you at home on that night?"

"Yes sir."

"How did your father get killed?" Horton asked.

"He was standing, pulling off his clothes, fixing to go to bed, and the shot came and he fell on the next bed, between there, and fell down," the child stammered.

Glenn described how his mother grabbed him and told him to take his baby brother and run from the house; how she ran out of the house and around back, near the well, screaming for help; how she was silenced by a gunshot.

"Is she dead now?"

The child stopped, looked down, detached, confused, numb. "Yes sir."

"Do you know how she got killed?"

"With a gun."

"Did you hear the gun fire?"

"Yes sir."

"Then what happened, James Glenn?"

"I jumped in the bed and somebody came in."

"Was the lamp light shining?"

"Yes."

"And somebody came in the house?"

"Yes, and blowed it out."

"Who was it that came into the house, if you know? What kind of looking person was he?"

"I didn't . . . I couldn't tell."

"Was he a white man or a black man?" Horton asked.

"I don't know," said Glenn.

"Did you see him start the fire?"

"No, ma'am." Glenn was confused, rattled. Horton pressed on, coaching his witness toward what he wanted the child to say, what they had in all likelihood already rehearsed.

"Did you see him put the light out?"

"Yes," the boy responded.

At the defense table Belden stood and interrupted. "If the Court please, we are going to ask him not to lead the witness all the way."

"The Court will allow you to lead the witness to some extent," said Judge Childers, "but don't lead the witness any more than you can help. He is of a very tender age, and it will be necessary to lead him some."

Horton continued. "James, you just tell the Court what happened after he blew the light out."

"Well, he blew the light out, and it sounded like he put on some clothes. He went out and set the side of the door afire, then I saw a black hand."

"Saw a hand?" Horton stopped and listened closely.

"A black hand," said Glenn. "And then the house was, it was light enough, I could see them go out again. I got the baby and ran off."

"Where did you go?"

"Down to the highway."

"What did you do when you got there?"

"I caught a ride," said Glenn.

"Where was your four-year-old brother when you left, Elvie Dean?"

"He was still in bed."

"He was still in bed?"

"Yes sir."

"What was Elvie Dean doing?"

"He was just laying in bed. I think he was already gone to sleep."

"Already gone to sleep?"

"Yes sir."

Horton took a seat at the prosecution table and Belden stood to cross-examine the boy. The packed courtroom, once raucous and whispering, was utterly silent.

"James, how close to either of these men were you?"

"I don't know."

"Just about how close? Will you tell me that, James?"

"About six inches."

"Do you understand how far six inches is? Will you measure it and show how far you think six inches is?" Belden asked.

"About that long," Glenn said, holding up his hands to indicate.

"You think they were that close to you? Do you think, James, that was one of them or both of them?" Belden asked.

"One. That blew out the lamp."

"They come into the room where you were, and you think he was about that far from you, is that right?"

"Yes sir."

"And the light, was it still burning when he came in?"

"Yes, and he blew it out."

"Did you see him before he came into the room?"

"Yes sir."

"Where were you?"

"But I didn't look," Glenn stammered, skipping a beat. "Yes, because I didn't look what color he was."

Belden paused. The boy had been through enough, he decided, and there was little more to be gained from the cross-examination. He had one final question. "Have the officers talked to you about this case a great many times?"

"I think just twice," said Glenn.

Belden excused the witness, and the court adjourned for the day.

That afternoon, Marshall and Belden went searching for a law library. There was vital new precedent upon which their defense of Lyons would hinge, and they needed a copy of a recent Supreme Court opinion to present at Lyons's trial. But a copy of the decision couldn't be found anywhere in the area. Before the close of business that day, Marshall rushed to send a telegram to the national NAACP office in New York: "In loose leaf blue notebook my desk is opinion by Justice Black in Chambers case from Florida. Send opinion Air Mail Special to Stanley Belden Webb Hotel Hugo Oklahoma. Case on trial. No library here."

5

WHEN JUDGE CHILDERS called the court back into session at 9:00 AM Tuesday morning, the courthouse and the grounds surrounding it were teeming again. But today the crowd was changed—there were white schoolchildren of all ages swarming everywhere, from fresh-faced elementary-aged children to high school kids on the precipice of adulthood. In just a few months many of them would graduate and ship off to war in Europe or in the Pacific.

Seizing on the opportunity to give the students a real-life lesson in the American legal system and to witness one of the most sensational news events ever to happen in sleepy Choctaw County, local authorities canceled classes for white children so the pupils could attend W.D. Lyons's murder trial. Black schools had either not been invited or had chosen not to allow their students to attend.

As he called the packed courtroom to order, Judge Childers welcomed the schoolchildren to his courtroom. "There are students here from Woodland and Grant and it's a gala day in a way for you, and I want not only to compliment these students for their order and decorum in this courtroom, but I want to compliment all of those who are here and are giving such close attention to this important trial."

A "gala day."

Marshall winced when the judge said that.

"Can you imagine a Negro on trial for his life being considered a 'gala day?'" he later wrote in a letter back to New York, stunned at the coldness of the statement, its implicit dehumanization of a living, breathing man whose life was on the line, and the racism ingrained so deeply within it that the white citizens listening probably didn't think twice about it. Still, he thought, there was an upside to the white schoolchildren in his audience for the day. "Those children were also given a lesson in constitutional law and rights of Negroes that they wouldn't get in their schools," he wrote. "I bet they have more respect for Negroes now."

The courtroom that morning bubbled over with chatter—of schoolchildren on a field trip excited to be out of class; of lawyers on both sides making their final preparations for the day's proceedings; and from the overflowing throng of onlookers waiting impatiently for the real spectacle that many had come to see. Marshall overheard someone in the crowd complain, "that nigger lawyer hasn't said anything."

On the morning of December 31, as the state presented the first part of its case, little in the basic facts was in dispute. L. B. Mills, who lived not far from Donna Scott's Cafe, testified to seeing Lyons in the Quarters that day with a package carried under his arm wrapped in newspaper. Sammie Green, who said he'd known W.D. Lyons "pretty near all my life," testified that one day, while they were clearing brush in Mr. Hall's pasture, Lyons asked if he might borrow his single-barrel shotgun sometime. Green said that on that New Year's Eve he'd lent Lyons the gun, the very gun the state had submitted into evidence. He could tell it was his gun because the hammer wouldn't stay cocked back.

"How do you shoot it?" county attorney Norman Horton asked when Green said that.

"Just pull the hammer and let it fall," Green said.

Green said that a day or two after New Year's, he'd traded Lyons a pocketknife for three unused 12-gauge shotgun shells.

Mrs. W. A. Hall, who with her husband owned the general store, testified that she'd known W.D. since he was a boy. On the day before New Year's Eve, she said, she saw W.D. Lyons and Van Bizzel at her store, where she sold Lyons six 12-gauge shotgun shells, an occurrence, she said, that was not at all unusual in the thirteen years she'd lived in Fort Towson.

Alton Ryder testified that he spent the day at Bus Fleeks's house in the Quarters, drinking wildcat, laughing, and talking. Throughout the day, he said, Lyons would stop in for a nip of whiskey, maybe five or six times in all.

Though these basic facts were not truly in dispute, Belden issued objections relentlessly, imploring Judge Childers to stop the county attorney from leading his witnesses, which Childers did, to little effect.

Horton called Dr. F. L. Waters to the stand, a physician who was present when x-rays were taken of the charred and broken corpses of Elmer and Marie Rogers. While Horton questioned his witness, Belden made objection after objection, asking that the testimony be thrown out because Waters had not supervised the taking of the x-rays; Dr. Johnson, who had, was sick that day and couldn't attend the trial. Attempting to circumvent that obstacle, Horton called to the stand the court stenographer who had been present at Lyons's preliminary hearing a year earlier to testify to the record he made that day, when Dr. Johnson had been present and able to discuss the x-rays of the bodies.

Here, Thurgood Marshall, who had been quiet up to now, made his first utterance before the court.

"If the Court please, may we ask a preliminary question before we raise an objection?"

"You may," Childers said.

"Mr. Reporter, does the record show whether or not W.D. Lyons was represented by counsel in this hearing from which you are now to read?"

"I think it does show," the court reporter responded.

"After reading that," Marshall said, "are you in a position to testify now whether or not he was represented by counsel at that hearing?"

"No sir, he was not."

"Now, Your Honor, please," Marshall said, turning toward the judge, "we object to the testimony on several grounds. In the first place, it was taken at a time when Lyons was not represented by counsel, had no opportunity for cross-examination, had no opportunity to consult said witness whose testimony is about to be read. It is fundamental law that the accused on trial is entitled to be confronted by witnesses and counsel have opportunity to cross-examine such witnesses." Marshall raised a whole litany of objections to the introduction of any evidence that had been first introduced at a time before Lyons was represented by a lawyer, though it would be more than twenty years before the US Supreme Court ruled in *Gideon v. Wainwright* that all criminal defendants have a constitutional right to an attorney.

The court reporter read from the transcript of the preliminary hearing, in which the defendants were asked if they wanted counsel. Van Bizzell asked to be represented by his chosen attorney. Lyons couldn't afford or find an attorney of his own, so the court appointed defense counsel for him. One after the next, each refused to represent him. When finally the pool of lawyers who might represent Lyons was exhausted, the preliminary hearing moved forward. Bizzell had a lawyer. Lyons, a barely literate farm-hand on trial for his life, had only himself.

Having established that fact in the record, Marshall let the prosecution continue. The state may have had an all-white jury and the specter of Jim Crow on its side, but it would still have to make its case for Lyons's guilt.

Horton called W. A. Hall to the stand. "What is your name?" Horton asked.

"W. A. Hall."

"What business are you in?"

"General mercantile."

"Did you see W.D. Lyons prior to the day the Rogers family was murdered?"

"I see him most every day, every two or three days," Hall said.

"When was the last time that you saw him before the murder?"

"I could not say exactly. He trades with me. This boy here was in there the Saturday before it happened."

"Which boy?" Horton asked.

"This boy here. What's his name?"

"Lyons."

"Lyons. He was coming back down the counter towards the grocery department to the ammunition."

"Did you ever sell him any shells?"

"Yes. I wanted to turn him down on account of his mother not being in shape, I was crediting her, to buy shells for him to hunt with."

"When did you sell him shells before?"

"I judge it to be, as nearly as I can remember, about six or eight months before. In other words, he was buying more shells, it was some time in hunting season, and he was buying more shells than I thought his mother ought to let him have on credit. I was crediting them."

"Do you know whether he was in town for six or eight months before then?"

Horton was alluding to Lyons's rap sheet as a small-time criminal (he was still serving a prison sentence for stealing chickens at the time in question), trying to surreptitiously get that otherwise irrelevant fact into the record.

Belden stood and spoke up to shut him down. "If the Court please, is the County Attorney trying to cross examine his own witness?"

"I don't know what he is trying to do," Judge Childers said.

A chastened Norman Horton excused the witness and called Oklahoma State Penitentiary warden Jess Dunn to the stand.

"Do you recall when the Rogers family was murdered at Fort Towson?"

"I do."

"What position did you hold at that time?"

"Warden of the Oklahoma State Penitentiary."

"Do you know W.D. Lyons, the defendant?"

"I do."

"When did you see him with reference to that murder?"

"He was brought into the penitentiary and into my office, I don't recall the date, or the time, but he was brought there by the then deputy sheriff, Van Raulston and Roy Marshall."

"Did you talk to the defendant?"

"Yes sir."

"Where did that conversation take place?"

"In the penitentiary, in my office."

"Who was present?"

"Raulston, Van, the deputy sheriff, and the barber from here, and Seals, chaplain of the penitentiary."

"Did you have a stenographer present to take down the conversation?"

"Yes."

"Mr. Dunn, I hand you State's Exhibit Nine," Horton said, handing Dunn a sheet of paper. "Will you identify that?"

"That is the statement that was taken in the office, in my office in the Oklahoma State Penitentiary. This is his signature that he signed, and this is his thumb print, finger and thumb print on this document."

"Was any force used on him?" Horton asked.

"Not one bit on earth," Dunn said.

"He made any promise?"

"No promise or threat. When they came to the penitentiary I told them to bring him to my office. I handled this boy before. I asked this boy did he want to make any kind of statement, and he said, 'Yes, I'll tell you all about it.' I went to questioning him and told the boy, I asked him was he afraid, and asked him was he afraid to talk in there. He said he was not, and he answered every question that I asked him, and I think the boy told the truth, just as it was."

Belden rose to his feet again. "Just a minute, now," he said. "We object to that and ask that it be stricken."

"The warden's opinion is not evidence in the case, gentlemen," Judge Childers said to the jury. "You will not consider it."

Marshall rose now.

"At this time we want to move that State's Exhibit Nine be not admitted into evidence at this time until the preliminary question is investigated on the statement made by the defendant, through counsel, that this statement, as well as any other that might be introduced, were made only after use of force and violence. We maintain that the statement is not voluntary and for that reason we ask the Court to excuse the jury so that we may go into the question of whether or not it is admissible under the law."

This was a crucial moment. Marshall had just introduced the team's first formal objection to Lyons's confession being admitted into evidence. Without this confession, the prosecution had only the wispiest ghost of a case: the child thought he saw a black hand, Lyons was black and had been seen in the area with a gun that day. Suppressing Lyons's confessions—both the one made in custody in Hugo and one made just twelve hours later in Jess Dunn's office in McAlester, was the essence of Lyons's defense strategy. And objecting on the record to those confessions being allowed into evidence would, in the likely event of a conviction by an all-white male jury in the Choctaw County courthouse, form the foundation of Lyons's appeal.

Having been roused from his sick bed, Doctor Johnson hobbled down to the courthouse, up the marble steps, and through the hall teeming with people to just outside the doors to the packed courtroom, where a fog of smoke hovered under the ceiling. County attorney Norman Horton was informed of his arrival and called his witness to the stand, but before Dr. Johnson could speak Marshall stood to raise another objection.

"Please the Court, for the sake of the record, the statement appeared that all witnesses were excused. Did that include Mr. Cheatwood or not?"

"I don't know Mr. Cheatwood," Judge Childers said.

"After he was excused from the rule over our objection, he is still in the courtroom and has been the whole time."

"You still urge your objection and ask that he be excluded?" Childers asked.

"We renew whatever objection we have that he should not have been in here. We renew it for purpose of the record," said Marshall.

"Is Mr. Cheatwood in the courtroom?" asked the judge.

Cheatwood spoke up from the gallery. "Yes sir."

"I believe I will excuse you from the courtroom," Childers said.

Cheatwood stood and shuffled through the packed room and out the doors into the hallway.

With Cheatwood gone, Childers allowed Johnson to offer brief testimony (essentially to tell the court that yes, the x-rays in question were those he had taken of bodies brought to him the day after the murder). The men of the jury were then ordered to stand and file out of the room while the court turned its attention to determining the admissibility of W.D. Lyons's confessions.

Stanley Belden called W.D. Lyons to the stand.

6

"**D**ID YOU OR did you not sign two statements?"

"I signed two statements," Lyons replied from his perch next to the judge in the witness stand, peering out over the crowded gallery with a now-empty jury box to his side.

"Did you do that of your own free will and voluntarily?"

"No sir."

Stanley Belden had his own client on the stand. Lyons's defense team was now in one of the most crucial phases of the trial, in which, without the jury present, they would seek to suppress the confessions Lyons had made on the grounds that they had been obtained through coercion. If they could accomplish this—if they could convince the judge that Lyons had confessed only after having been beaten and tortured until he would say anything to make his tormentors stop—then the state's case would unravel like an old rope, and they wouldn't have to rest their hopes on the odds that the all-white jury might give an impartial examination of the evidence stacked up against a black man accused of murdering a white child and his white mother and father. If they could do this they might just win.

"You state in your own way to the Court what took place after you were arrested," Belden said.

"When they arrested me at my home, two officers arrested me when I came home one night. As they was bringing me down Jefferson Street they started beating me."

"What officers?"

"One was Reasor Cain. The other one, I didn't know his name."

Horton interjected. "We object as incompetent, irrelevant, and immaterial, and not going to the exhibit that the State has offered in evidence."

"It might go to the condition of the defendant's mind," Judge Childers said. "He has a right to state what treatment he received while in the custody of the officers."

Horton pressed further, sensing how much was at stake in this particular line of questioning. "I believe something they claim was done to the defendant on a prior occasion to the time he made the confession we offer is immaterial. If they can prove threats and violence made at the approximate time this confession was made, that would be admissible, but to go back and show a former course of conduct had at another time, by other people, or another occasion, than the people before whom he made this confession, is not admissible. If they show that the people before whom he made this confession mistreated him, that would be admissible."

"The law," Belden said, "is that a confession obtained under duress, force, or threats, if a confession is obtained under those conditions, and a later confession is obtained, that later confession is no more competent to be introduced than the first, if a defendant has undergone those experiences before he makes any confession."

"Have you a citation on that?" the judge asked.

"Yes sir," said Belden.

"Let's hear it," said Judge Childers.

Horton interrupted again, raising the same objection as before. Judge Childers scolded him.

"You lose sight of the Court's idea of the proposition about his state of mind," Childers said, "which might have been created in the boy's mind by something done prior to that. He might not have known the differences in the officers that held him then and the officers that held him before. He might have been in that state of mind, I don't know, and I want to find out if his mind had been placed in the condition that placed fear through his mind through the whole time. I want him to have a trial according to the law and the evidence in the case. That is my sworn duty, to see that he gets it. That is what I want to see that he gets. Go ahead and read that law."

Marshall's heart rate must have climbed with his spirits. Here was Judge Childers, representative in Choctaw County of American jurisprudence itself, not just stating that he wanted Lyons to get a fair trial but coming to within a hair of making Marshall's case for him. If coerced confessions are inadmissible, and a beating that came well before a confession still amounts to coercion, then Lyons's second confession—the one given twelve hours after the beating stopped, the one obtained within the walls of the Oklahoma State Penitentiary now being offered in evidence by the district attorney—would be inadmissible. Marshall, newly confident and ready to trot out the Supreme Court precedent he himself had helped establish just a year earlier, explained the case law to the judge.

"I found out on coming here that there is no library available, but I know the exact title of the case I refer to, *Dave Canty v. State of Alabama*, decided in the United States Supreme Court about March 1940, about two or three weeks after the decision of a case in Florida [the *Chambers* case]. That case was reversed and the State was not permitted to argue it. There was no opinion but memorandum, and the facts are essentially these: Canty was in prison in Alabama. He was taken from Kilby prison to Montgomery and taken to the police station and beaten severely. After he was beaten practically to the extent that he did not know what he was doing, they asked him if he was ready to confess. He said he would say anything to keep from being beaten. They carried him back to the penitentiary at Kilby, and they had the warden and a group of citizens who knew nothing about the beating in Montgomery. Canty was asked in the presence of witnesses, Do you want to make a statement? Canty said yes. They asked him, Are you making this statement of your free will and voluntarily, and he said yes. I submit that that case was reversed on the brief of Chambers, which showed force and violence were used, and the facts are close. He was not beaten at the Kilby prison. The beating took place miles away, in Montgomery, Alabama, and the court reversed that case saying that force and violence could not be used. As I said before, there is no opinion, there is merely a memorandum, and the facts as I have given them are, as nearly as I can recollect, the record of the case, and I am familiar with them, for I prepared the petition for the writ of certiorari. It is awfully close to this case."

Judge Childers replied not to Marshall but to Lyons, glancing down to the witness seated below him. His simple response carried implications that would echo through the lives of many in the courtroom that day, and untold others across America over the decades that followed.

"I will permit you to testify," he said.

───────────

His own first-person account of what had happened to him during his arrest and interrogation would be the cornerstone of Lyons's defense, as the legal team leaned on the precedent Marshall had created with his groundbreaking victory in the United States Supreme Court a year earlier in *Chambers v. Florida*. In *Chambers*, Marshall argued that the confessions extracted from his clients—four poor black men from a group of around forty the authorities initially rounded up in their investigation into the robbery and murder of an elderly white man—were inadmissible as evidence on the grounds that they had been obtained through coercion. The men had been held for days without charges or access to visitors or an attorney, isolated from the world and intimidated until they admitted that they killed the man.

The strategy Marshall decided on in the *Chambers* case was a risky one. Though just a few years before, in *Brown v. Mississippi*, the high court had tossed out the confessions of three black men whom the authorities freely admitted they'd whipped and beaten with extreme cruelty (one was strung up by the neck, as if to lynch him), in *Chambers*, the defendants had not been physically tortured. Nonetheless, Marshall contended, their confessions had been coerced. The defendants had been held without counsel for a week, aggressively interrogated, and frightened to the same ends that authorities might beat or maim a suspect: to fray his nerves and break his will.

In a decision handed down on February 12, 1940, for the first time the high court ruled that Section 1 of the Fourteenth Amendment to the US Constitution—". . . nor shall any State deprive any person of life, liberty, or property, without due process of law . . ."—compelled the states and not just the federal government to abide by due process procedures and traditions. Writing for a unanimous court, former Ku Klux Klan member Justice Hugo Black declared that the record of events "shows, without conflict, the dragnet methods of arrest on suspicion without warrant, and the protracted questioning and cross-questioning of these ignorant young colored tenant farmers by state officers and other white citizens, in a fourth floor jail room, where, as prisoners, they were held without friends, advisers or counselors, and under circumstances calculated to break the strongest nerves and the stoutest resistance." In his decision,

Black dwelled on the fact that the defendants had been held for days on end without charges and with little sleep, under circumstances specifically designed to fill them "with terror and frightful misgivings."

Though the United States had yet to get drawn into the conflict, mere months earlier Nazi Germany had invaded Poland, and by January 1940 inklings were beginning to emerge of the camps to which the Third Reich was sending Jews, dissidents, and others whom the Nazis considered enemies of the state. In words that fellow Supreme Court justice Felix Frankfurter called "one of the enduring utterances in the history of the Supreme Court and in the annals of human freedom," Justice Black wrote:

> Today, as in ages past, we are not without tragic proof that the exalted power of some governments to punish manufactured crime dictatorially is the handmaid of tyranny. Under our constitutional system, courts stand against any winds that blow as havens of refuge for those who might otherwise suffer because they are helpless, weak, outnumbered, or because they are nonconforming victims of prejudice and public excitement. Due process of law, preserved for all by our Constitution, commands that no such practice as that disclosed by this record shall send any accused to his death. No higher duty, no more solemn responsibility, rests upon this Court than that of translating into living law and maintaining this constitutional shield deliberately planned and inscribed for the benefit of every human being subject to our Constitution—of whatever race, creed or persuasion.

From the witness stand, with Judge Childers looming over him, Lyons looked out at his lawyers and into a courtroom gallery packed with the people of Choctaw County. Some of them he'd known his entire life. Some were friends, others mere acquaintances. Some were strangers. There were blacks and whites, some old, some young like him, and some just children. Lyons must have felt the weight of the moment pressing down upon him that day as he faced the people of Hugo and the surrounding towns, his people, all sitting bunched up next to one another, blacks on one side, whites on another, all silent, looking back at him, while he delivered a bone-chilling account of his treatment at the hands of the police in their community.

On Thursday, January 11, Lyons was at his mother-in-law's house in Hugo, where he'd been living. As the sun was settling on the horizon Lyons ducked outside. It was cold and he wore no jacket, just a shirt and overalls over another pair of pants, but he planned to be outside for only a few minutes. He walked over to a spot near the railroad tracks where he kept some whiskey hidden away to have a swig from the clear, cold jar.

As he made his way home, his chest still warm with the burn of white whiskey, Lyons met a boy on the road. There was a group of cars at his mother-in-law's house, he said. Maybe three.

"Might be the laws," said the boy.

Lyons asked him to run back down to the house to see what was going on. He was nervous. He'd been hunting lately without a license, and anyway, he'd been in trouble with the law before and he'd known others who looked like him who'd gotten mixed up with the authorities too. It often didn't end well.

The boy left, but he never came back. Lyons stood in the cold for a while, waiting for the boy to return, shivering without a jacket. Finally he decided to go on home to see for himself what was afoot.

Lyons opened the front door to his mother-in-law's house and walked inside. Reasor Cain, a railroad detective Lyons recognized from around town, raised his gun and ordered him to put his hands in the air. Another officer, Oscar Bearden, who was unknown to Lyons, stood from hiding behind the stove with his gun raised, walked over to Lyons, and pressed his pistol against his body.

Bearden handed his gun to Cain and reached into Lyons's overalls. He undid the belt that held up Lyons's pants beneath and yanked it out through the belt loops, ordering Lyons to put his hands behind his back. While Cain stood with a gun in each hand pointed at Lyons and his wife stood by frozen and confused, Bearden ran the belt around Lyons's hands, pulled it tight, and secured the buckle. Cain returned Bearden his gun. With his arms stretched back tight and his hands bound together, Lyons felt the barrel of a pistol press into his back as Bearden forced him outside into the bracing cold. Reasor Cain followed.

The night was a thin darkness with no moon and all moisture drawn into crisp layers of ice on the trees and grass. Their steps crunching carefully on the quiet streets, where patches of ice hid in the shadows, Bearden and Cain marched Lyons north toward Jefferson Street. With his gun pressed into Lyons's back, Bearden punched him in the head. Lyons crumbled to the ground, shrieking in pain.

"Shut up that hollering," Bearden said, swinging a kick into Lyons's body. He spied a wooden board by the side of the road and told Cain to break him off a piece, yanking Lyons up from the ground and forcing him further down the road. They approached Jefferson Street, a main thoroughfare through town, and Bearden swung his new club into Lyons's forehead with a thwack above the right eye. Lyons fell again. Bearden kicked him before pulling him back to his feet.

The courthouse came into view, illuminated with the warm glow of streetlamps just a block away, but before they reached the light Bearden grabbed Lyons and pushed him up against a tree in the shadows by the side of the road, smacking his head against the bark, and promised to kill Lyons slowly if he didn't confess.

"He told Reasor Cain to come over here and get some more officers, and we'll drag him through colored town and let the rest of the Negroes learn a lesson," Lyons said to the hushed courtroom. The crowd listened pensively as Lyons recounted the beating that took place just steps from where they then sat in silent thrall. From the courthouse steps they could see where Bearden had pressed Lyons into a tree and thrust fear of death, or worse, into his heart.

Cain left the two men at the tree and attempted to assemble a posse—for what purpose was unclear, which may have been the point. Whether he truly intended to lynch Lyons or just wanted to instill the fear of a lynching in him, Cain couldn't round up enough men for the job. Instead, Lyons was taken to the courthouse and turned over to Deputy Sheriff Floyd Brown and the jailer, Leonard Holmes. As they dragged Lyons to the top floor of the courthouse, to the women's section of the jail, Sheriff Brown kicked and punched him. Holmes, the jailer, swung his heavy leaden keychain into Lyons's face, striking his teeth with a dull clang and busting his lip. They tossed him in a cell, and as word spread that "the laws" had found their man, the officers who had been working on the case rushed to the courthouse.

After just five minutes alone, with blood streaming down his face, his right eye and lips swelling, and his head aching from the blows, Lyons heard the door to his cell swing open. Leonard Holmes grabbed him and, with help from Sheriff Brown, walked him back down the stairs to the bottom floor of the jail, into a room connected to Brown's office, where more law enforcement officers sat waiting, including a deputy sheriff and a heavyset highway patrolman. Lyons knew many of these men by name— they were neighbors, of a kind, after all—and he knew all of them by sight, except one. The unknown man had crooked teeth and doughy features and wore a dour expression on his face. He dressed differently than the others, with a dark suit vest and a full-length single-breasted overcoat on his trim frame. Rather than the cattleman-style cowboy hats favored by men in southeastern Oklahoma, he wore a fedora with a hat band and the brim cocked up in the back, turned down in front. He was, a local observer might have remarked, a city slicker—the special investigator dispatched to town from Oklahoma City by Governor Phillips himself to assist with the case: Vernon Cheatwood.

The lawmen laid into Lyons with renewed savagery, slamming his head against the wall and taking turns punching and kicking the suspect in the face, stomach, and ribs. Lyons crumpled to the floor, but they forced him up, ordering him to stand against the wall with his hands raised above his head. Wearing cowboy boots, Cheatwood kicked Lyons in the legs until the skin peeled off his shins, leaving them bloody and raw.

"What did they threaten?" Stanley Belden asked his client on the witness stand. "Tell the court what they said." The room was entranced.

"'You goddamned son of a bitch,'" Lyons said, impersonating a nameless, faceless stand-in for all of his tormentors, "'you committed that crime and you are going to tell us.' I told them I didn't know anything about what crime. They went to beating me harder and kept beating me for about two hours. Then they carried me to the jail house and didn't bother me for eleven days."

His ordeal had only just begun.

7

THE CONCEPT OF "stress" as a discrete aspect of human psychology was borrowed from engineering, where its meaning is explicit, unambiguous, and instructive: the load an object experiences when subjected to force. For the engineer, stress is a key concept because accounting for the amount of stress experienced by any given part of a structure is essential in order to ensure that the entire edifice is structurally sound. More to the point, stress is a key metric for determining the point at which a structure or material will reach "ultimate failure," in engineering jargon, which is to say, in laymen's terms, its breaking point.

Understanding the effect stress has on the human body is not as simple as measuring how excited or frightened a person becomes. It involves looking at the specific ways that stress manifests—looking at the forces exerted upon the elements that altogether form a sane human mind—particularly as they relate to the point at which the mind reaches ultimate failure. Put another way, understanding how stress works requires understanding how and why a person might finally crack, which is the ultimate purpose of torture as an interrogation technique.

The human body's first response to a highly stressful situation is to release a whole host of hormones produced by the adrenal glands. The two most important among them are epinephrine, which causes the heart rate and breathing to accelerate (preparing you to fight or run like hell), and cortisol, an anti-inflammatory hormone that helps keep blood sugar and electrolyte levels in balance, among other things. In the near term, cortisol helps with short-term memory formation, but prolonged exposure to high levels of cortisol in the body actually has the opposite effect, damaging the hippocampus and impairing memory formation. Raised cortisol levels over time have been observed alongside serious depression, anxiety disorders, and a generally decreased resilience to psychological stress. High levels of stress over time often lead to the adrenal glands and the amygdala becoming enlarged, creating a negative feedback loop in which the more excitable a brain is, the more sensitive it is to stressful stimuli, and thus less resilient to stress. Experiencing stress does not, in itself, make a person tougher or inured to its effects, but the opposite. The net effect of high stress over time tends to be confusion, disorientation, and a damaged, vulnerable mind.

People routinely underestimate their ability to endure physical pain and discomfort while overestimating their ability to endure mental and emotional torment. Though the beating meted out to W.D. Lyons by Vernon Cheatwood and the lawmen of Choctaw County was exceptionally painful, it was not the worst part of his ordeal. As behavioral science researcher Shane O'Mara explains, "Predator stress—the physiological and psychological stress experienced when your life is threatened—is perhaps the most extreme form of stress that it is possible to experience."

While W.D. Lyons spent eleven days in a jail cell above the courthouse—bruised, bloody, and fearing for his life—he was not at rest. Though the physical beatings had stopped, for the moment, the torture of W.D. Lyons had not. In every moment that he lay alone on the floor of his cell, his lip fat and busted, his nose encrusted with coagulated blood, his eye socket inflamed and swollen shut, his shoulder throbbing, his ribs badly bruised if not broken, for all the pain that pulsated through his head, limbs, and torso, the worst part was the protracted fear, the utter powerlessness, the shock and foreboding sense of doom that loomed over his every moment. One second he'd been at home with his wife and mother-in-law when he slipped out of the house to take of nip of whiskey in the woods—the next he was accused of a heinous murder and entirely at the mercy of violent men who had threatened to take his life and had already proven themselves willing to beat him within inches of it.

Those eleven quiet days W.D. Lyons spent in the jail above the courthouse were mostly made up of hours upon hours of silence and isolation, but he did have visitors. Lawmen came to question him "once or twice," Lyons said, as he sat in the witness stand facing the captivated courtroom. Nearly a year to the day from the events he was recounting, he couldn't recall exactly how many times he was questioned during that delirious week and a half. Soon after his arrest, his wife and sister came to visit, but they talked of very little. They could see plainly the bruises that covered his face, arms, and back, and it was easy enough to surmise what had happened to him. Mostly they just embraced, and the two women helped Lyons to stand and walk a bit; when they arrived they found him lying on the ground and he was only able to stand by hoisting himself up with his arms around the women's shoulders.

On Monday evening, January 22, Lyons was removed from his jail cell and taken to the office of county attorney Norman Horton—the very man now leading the case against him, watching from the prosecution table as he testified. On the way there, a highway patrol officer began striking him on the back of the head with a blackjack. When Vernon Cheatwood saw this he ordered the highway patrolman to stop—"I know how to get it out of him when we get him up here," Cheatwood said, according to Lyons. Once at Horton's office, Cheatwood handcuffed Lyons to a chair and stood imposingly in front of him. Norman Horton, Lyons said, was sitting to his left, while detective Reasor Cain was behind him and the heavyset highway patrolman was to his right.

"Mr. Cheatwood called me a black son of a bitch, and threatened to stick red hot irons to me to make me confess to a crime," Lyons said. "Mr. Cheatwood was saying: 'Didn't you commit the crime?' I told him no. Mr. Cheatwood was yelling, 'Why don't you answer the prosecutor's question?' And he was beating on me all that time."

"How was he beating you?" Belden asked.

"Beating me with a blackjack. He was sitting in front of me, whipping me on the legs and knees and hands, and shoulders and arms."

"What kind of blackjack was that?" said Belden.

"It was a flat one, loaded with some kind of shot, because every time he hit me it rattled inside. Shaped something like a milk bottle. The first lick he struck me was the back part of my head."

"Who was that?" asked Belden.

"The heavyset highway patrolman," Lyons said. "Reasor Cain was behind me. He beat me with his fist behind my head, then he would pull my hair, then he would shake my head, and hit me with his fist every once in a while, and Mr. Cheatwood he was hitting me and beating me in front, on the knees and legs and arms and shoulders with the blackjack. And they taken me up several times on a table like this, taken me across it and whipped me on the back. One would beat me for an hour and a half or two, then he would get tired, and the other would take me, and beat me that way all night."

Not long after midnight the lawmen placed a pan in Lyons's lap. In it were bones and bone fragments, like a piece of a jawbone with the teeth still attached.

"They said they were the bones of Mrs. Rogers, Mr. Rogers, and the baby," Lyons told the court, "and I had never seen any bones of a dead person before, had I ever seen dead people before, and I was afraid of those bones on my lap in the pan. Mr. Cheatwood would lay the bones on my hands, such as teeth and body bones, and make me hold it and look at it, wouldn't let me turn my head away, and beat me on the hands and knees."

The beatings carried on for hours, lawmen beating on Lyons in unison and separately, taking turns as they exhausted themselves, shouting at him, demanding that he admit to the Rogers murders. As he had when he was first arrested, when they beat him against a tree and raised the specter of a lynching, when they beat him at the jail, when they left him for days writhing in pain on the floor, Lyons denied any connection to the crime—until finally, at roughly 4:30 in the morning on Tuesday, January 23, approximately ten hours into this particular round of torture, twelve days after he was taken into custody, W.D. Lyons broke.

"Tell the court what took place then," Belden said.

"Beat me and beat me until I couldn't stand no more, until I gave in to them and answered the questions they demanded."

"Tell the court what that question was."

"They asked me did I kill Mr. Elmer Rogers."

"Who asked that?"

"Mr. Prosecutor."

"Do you mean Mr. Horton, the county attorney?"

"Yes sir."

"What did you say?"

"I told him no. Then Mr. Cheatwood hit me again with the same blackjack. He come and told me, 'Lyons, you old black son of a bitch,' and told me I was lying, told me I'd better answer those questions, or either I takes some more beating. They started beating me some more, and yelled to me to answer the prosecutor's questions."

"What did you say to that?" Belden said.

"I said yes."

"You said yes?"

"Yes sir."

"Were they beating on you at that time?"

"Yes sir."

"Who was beating you?"

"Mr. Cheatwood."

"Was it true that you had killed Elmer Rogers?"

"No sir."

"Why did you say you had?"

"Because I was forced to."

"What do you mean by you was forced to?"

"I was beat with a blackjack, tortured all night long."

"Why did you say yes?"

"Because I feared I would get some more torture."

———————

Sheriff Roy Harmon pulled W.D. Lyons's mangled, bloodied body up from the chair in the county attorney's office—he couldn't stand on his own—and carried him back to the jail section of the courthouse. Lyons stayed in a cell there for just five minutes before men returned and brought him to the sheriff's office. If one assumes Lyons woke up sometime in the morning on Monday and was awake most of the day until the beatings began, he had now been without sleep for approaching twenty-four hours. The lawmen ate breakfast while he sat in a chair and waited, perhaps nodding off, until they loaded him into a car.

As dawn began to glow on the horizon, a deputy sheriff, highway patrolman, assistant county attorney, and Vernon Cheatwood packed into a car with Lyons and drove twenty minutes or so from Hugo east down Highway 70 toward the charred remains of the Rogers farmhouse. A thin sheet of snow had fallen over the fields and roads of Choctaw County, still fresh and white, untrammeled in the new morning.

"They told me they was taking me down there to kill me," Lyons said from the witness stand.

"Which one said that?" asked Belden.

"Mr. Cheatwood asked me didn't I want to say my prayers."

When they arrived at the site where once stood the Rogerses' home, all that remained of the structure was its chimney. On the morning after the fire, the soot-covered bricks, charred fragments, and ashes of the building's footprint had been raked to the perimeter of the structure, and now stood out sharply, like a black stamp smudged on the snow-white field. The men made a fire for warmth, promising Lyons, who stood handcuffed next to it, that they'd use it to burn him if he didn't stick to his confession. A rotating cast of men shuffled among the ruins—even Vernon Colclasure, the brother of the slain Mrs. Rogers, was brought to the scene—apparently searching for something. It had been twenty-three days since Elmer, Marie, and four-year-old Elvie Dean Rogers were murdered and their home burned to the ground.

"When I turned around," Lyons said from the stand, "Mr. Harvey Hawkins had an ax in his hand. He went to saying I knowed something about it. I told him I didn't know nothing about it. They said they got it out of the ashes."

Lyons described how the men questioned him over and over about the ax blade he insisted he knew nothing about, as they went through the motions of a proper investigation. They demanded he tell them where he'd been rabbit hunting on New Year's Eve, and Lyons showed them the spot a half mile away where he'd fired his gun. They found two spent shotgun shells on the ground, which they collected as evidence. As the sun climbed toward the apex of the sky and the soft morning glow gave way to brittle sunshine, the lawmen loaded Lyons into the car and took him back to jail.

That evening, the assistant county attorney, the court clerk, and Vernon Cheatwood came to Lyons's cell with a written statement, ordering him to sign him it. He asked what it was.

"Never mind," Cheatwood told him. "I said go ahead and sign your name on it."

After nearly two days without sleep, amid repeated rounds of beatings and constant threats, Lyons signed their statement. With their confession in hand the lawmen walked Lyons out into the jail yard and posed for pictures with him, like trophy hunters commemorating a kill.

After that, Lyons was transported to the Oklahoma State Penitentiary at McAlester, a drive of a little more than an hour, where his captors sat him in a chair in the office of the prison warden Jess Dunn and ordered him to tell the warden what he'd told them.

"They went to accusing—Mr. Van Raulston was accusing me of the crime," Lyons said from the witness stand, "said I committed it, and was telling me how the crime happened, and I was still answering no. Then Mr. Van Raulston said, 'You either answer our questions or get treated like you was down at Hugo.' He beat me awhile longer, until I couldn't stand it anymore, I was already hurting from—already hurting from that last night beating, I hadn't had any sleep since that Sunday night. It was Tuesday night then. Mr. Van Raulston asked me was I ready to answer his question, and I told him yes, and Mr. Dunn and Mr. Van Raulston was telling me how the crime happened."

Lyons signed a statement prepared for him by his captors. "I, W.D. Lyons, a negro," the statement read, "at 8:15 o'clock P. M., on this the 23rd day of January, 1940, in the office of Warden J. F. Dunn at the Oklahoma State Penitentiary at McAlester, in the presence of . . . etc. etc." Dunn ordered he be taken to the basement of the prison—the "death cells," Lyons called them in his testimony—to a cell mere feet from "Old Sparky," the nickname given by prison officials to the electric chair. "Mr. Dunn told me he had done sent down thirty-nine men," Lyons said.

"Sent them where?" Belden asked his client.

"To death in the electric chair."

"What else was said, if anything?" Belden asked.

"Then he told me if I wouldn't plead guilty, then I would be the fortieth one. Then I got scared. I thought he was going to kill me sure enough."

In his testimony to the court, W.D. Lyons told of how he was left overnight in a cell on death row near the electric chair. In the morning he was taken to another cell elsewhere in the prison, and the morning after brought to the warden's office before his preliminary hearing. He testified that Vernon Cheatwood was there, that Cheatwood threatened to kill him if he didn't plead guilty, that he insisted on his innocence again, and that he received another beating from Cheatwood's blackjack. He testified that Warden Dunn threatened to hang him by his handcuffs from the ceiling if he didn't confess before he was finally brought back to Hugo for his preliminary hearing to the very courtroom where he now sat facing many of the men who had taken part in his ordeal.

Belden excused his client, and one of those very men stood to challenge Lyons's story

"Now, W.D., you seem to be very bitter in naming some of the officers you say mistreated you," county attorney Norman Horton said standing before W.D. Lyons in the witness stand. "Now you say, going back to that time they got you out of jail at six thirty, you say they brought you to my office?"

"Yes sir," Lyons replied.

"And you say I was there?"

"That is right."

"Don't you know that I did not come to the office until ten o'clock that night?"

Lyons looked Horton square in the eyes. "You were in the office that night," he said defiantly. The audience tittered.

"I was not in the office when you first came to the office, was I?" Horton insisted.

"You were there until they stopped beating me," Lyons said. The tension grew palpably in the packed courtroom, and Horton was growing agitated.

"I wasn't there in the office until six thirty was I, when they beat you? Isn't it true that Vernon Cheatwood had a strap of leather, and was tapping you like that?" Horton said, leaning in, and softly tapping his hand in the air. Horton sharpened his voice and looked into Lyons's eyes. "And because you refused to answer questions they put to you?"

At the defense table Stanley Belden leaped to his feet to raise an objection.

"Don't intimidate the witness," Judge Childers admonished the county attorney, "just use the ordinary tone of voice."

Lyons spoke next. "That blackjack was loaded," he said.

"How do you know it was loaded?" Horton asked. "You were insolent to the officers, and sat and sulked when I asked you questions, isn't that true?"

"No sir."

"Isn't it true that you refused to answer, and they struck you on the knee with a piece of leather?"

"They struck me all night. I didn't rest any."

"You told me that night where you hid the ax, didn't you?"

"No sir."

"They didn't beat into you where you hid that ax, under the house, did they?"

"No sir."

"And you say you did not go out in the morning after you were in the county attorney's office and show the officers who had been looking for three weeks for the ax, and go to the place and show them, under the window, after you had shot that woman, chopped her ribs out, and knocked her teeth out, and show them where that ax was found, where it was buried in the ground?"

"I didn't show them any ax."

"Why did you want to accuse Van Bizzell?"

"Because the officers forced me to accuse him," Lyons said.

"Forced you to accuse another man, did they?" Horton said, cheekily. "They didn't make you say Van Bizzell was with you, did they?"

"Sure they did."

"Isn't it true that after they got through hitting you, as you say, with a strap of leather, and you refused to answer any questions at all times, that I made them stop whipping you, and told them to get out of the room, and I asked you if you wouldn't talk to me alone? Isn't that right?"

Thurgood Marshall stirred inside. There it was—the county attorney, on the record, admitting that the lawmen of Choctaw County had whipped W.D. Lyons. It wasn't everything, far from it, but it was something.

"When you were talking to me alone, didn't Roy Harmon come in?" Horton said.

"I didn't talk to you alone," said Lyons.

"Didn't you make a statement to me and Roy Harmon, when Cheatwood wasn't there, and Hawkins wasn't there, and Raulston, and you told us you killed the people, and where you put the ax?"

"No sir."

"You deny that now?"

"That is right," Lyons said.

Horton excused the witness.

———————

With Lyons's testimony complete, Belden moved to have his confession suppressed owing to "the force and violence used by the various officers with a blackjack, beating and kicking, and other means of violence . . ."

Horton interjected. "We would like to offer a little evidence in support of our response."

"It will be permitted," said the judge.

———————

One after the next Horton called the law enforcement officers who had been involved in apprehending Lyons to the stand. The first of them, Roy Harmon, who had been sheriff when Lyons was arrested, testified that the defendant had confessed of his own free will, as would each of the lawmen who testified after him. But it was in this moment, after the prosecution finished questioning Sheriff Harmon and it was the defense's turn to question the witness, that Marshall and Belden initiated the second phase of their strategy. Belden remained seated and Thurgood Marshall, standing tall, trim, and confident—the first African American attorney that most if not all people in the courtroom had ever seen—approached Harmon on the witness stand.

Marshall aggressively challenged Harmon's side of the story, and the sheriff was evasive, insisting he never saw Lyons being beaten and that he couldn't remember details of the ordeal. The defense team was trying to establish for the record who had been present while Lyons was being interrogated. But a year had passed since then, and Harmon shielded himself with strategic ambiguity—he couldn't be sure, or couldn't remember, or could only say what he saw.

"Did there come a time when you had a picture taken with him near the jail?" Marshall asked.

"Yes."

"Would you recognize that picture if you saw it again?"

"I should think so," Harmon replied.

Marshall produced an enlarged copy of the picture taken with the lawmen and Lyons after his confession. If Harmon wouldn't cop to even being present during key points of Lyons's interrogation, then Marshall would undermine the believability of his testimony.

"Mr. Harmon, I ask you if this is a reprint of the picture you just mentioned?"

"I don't know."

"Do you know these people shown in the reprint?" Marshall asked.

"I can't tell very much about it."

"Do you know who this is?"

"Looks a little like me but there are several fellows here that favor me."

The absurdity of the state's case against Lyons was growing unsustainable. The courtroom audience laughed openly as the former sheriff claimed he couldn't recognize his own image in the picture, and Judge Childers admonished the crowd to be silent, threatening to clear the courtroom if there were more disruptions.

"Who does that look like in the middle?" Marshall asked, pointing to the image of his client surrounded by white men on both sides.

"These negroes look nearly alike to me, can't hardly tell them apart," Harmon said.

Belden stood and tried his hand with the witness.

"Would you say that that is not you?" Belden asked.

"I didn't say it wasn't me," said Harmon.

"What is your honest opinion?"

"I said it looked like me."

"Does it look like W.D. Lyons?"

"I said I can't tell these negroes apart," Harmon said.

"Does that look like Mr. Cheatwood?"

"It resembles him some. You see that shades him."

Belden returned to the defense table, and Marshall took over again to deliver the final blow to Harmon's credibility. "Mr. Harmon," Marshall said, "is W.D. Lyons in the courtroom now?"

"W.D. Lyons?" Harmon said. "Yes."

"Can you point him out?"

"Yes."

"Where is he?" Marshall asked, poised like a hunter with his prey in the crosshairs.

"Sitting over there."

Marshall let his reply hang in the air as he returned to his seat at the defense table. "I thought they all looked alike," he said.

"Why did they put the pan of bones in his lap?" Belden asked.

"I figure it was to get him to thinking about what he did," former deputy sheriff Floyd Brown replied from the witness stand.

"You were trying to get a confession, weren't you?"

"That was the purpose of it, yes."

"And you know that most colored people are superstitious and afraid of the dead, and that was the purpose of putting those bones in his lap, was to frighten him, wasn't it?"

"Well, I don't know," Brown said. "Some of them don't frighten very easily. But it might help a good bit."

"And in your opinion, with a good many colored people, that would help, wouldn't it?"

"Yes," Brown said, "and a few white people, too."

Notwithstanding their casual racism, the lawmen were all skilled witnesses, experienced and comfortable on the stand. One after the next, they took the stand to deny ever hurting Lyons during the investigation, asserting, rightly, that they could only testify to what they'd seen, and at other times saying they simply couldn't remember.

But Belden and Marshall took turns chiseling at the cracks in the testimony of each. Belden pointed out that the county attorney himself, earlier that very day, had said he stopped officers from whipping Lyons. He got former deputy sheriff Floyd Brown to admit seeing Cheatwood hit Van Bizzell during his interrogation. And he got Brown to freely admit that the officers had used the bones of a dead woman, her dead husband, and their child to frighten Lyons.

With that, the defense completed its argument, made without the jury present, that W.D. Lyons's confessions were obtained through coercion.

Judge Childers issued his decision as to whether or not the confessions could be considered by the jury.

"Let the record show," he said, "that the Court finds that the defendant may have been frightened into making the confession that was made here in the courthouse, by long hours of questioning and by placing bones of the purported bodies of the deceased persons on his lap during the questioning. The first confession, made in the courthouse at Hugo is by the Court ruled out. The second confession, made at McAlester, the Court finds that the weight of the evidence in that matter indicates that no threats were made, that no offer of leniency was held out, that the confession was made voluntarily by the defendant, and is admitted in evidence. The Court will take recess until nine o'clock in the morning."

Judge Childers stood and exited through back of the courtroom, into his chambers. W.D. Lyons said his goodbyes to Dunjee and his attorneys and went with the bailiff back upstairs to the jail cell where he'd been living now for more than a year.

As the attorneys and the rest of the crowd filed out of the packed and smoky courtroom, Marshall was surprised when he took note that whispers and sneers echoing into the hallway were directed not at him but at Norman Horton and the other state's witnesses who had taken the stand that day. Some even told the lawmen outright what they thought of them—"some mighty nasty comments," as Marshall later wrote in a letter—while others stopped Marshall and Belden in the hall to tell them they were enjoying the spectacle and complimented their performance. Nearly everyone, it seemed, black and white alike, believed W.D. Lyons to be innocent. For the first time since taking on Lyons as a client, Thurgood Marshall—who was well accustomed to losing in southern courtrooms—confronted an unfamiliar prospect. Ever since taking the case he'd planned to appeal the verdict, assuming his client could never win in Little Dixie, but something seemed to be shifting in the ground beneath him. With the witnesses he planned to call the next day—four white citizens of Choctaw County whose testimony he hoped would erode what authority there was left in the testimony of local officials—he thought maybe he could win this thing.

8

January 29, 1941

"GENTLEMEN OF THE JURY," Belden began. "In this case, the defendant believes the facts to be as I am going to relate to you now."

Standing before the twelve white men of the jury, now back in the courtroom, Belden recounted for them the events as Lyons had reported them, from the moment a group of lawmen showed up at his house while he was off sipping whiskey by the railroad tracks, through his beatings and other torments—sleep deprivation, the pan of bones, the electric chair—and finally to his confessions.

"Gentlemen of the jury, if we produce these facts," he said, "as we will, we are going to ask at your hands an acquittal, that you find in your verdict that the defendant is not guilty of the crime that he is charged with."

Earlier in the day, prosecutors had presented their own case in front of the jury, essentially a repeat of the case they made to Judge Childers as they argued that Lyons's second confession—the one made several hours after his worst beatings had ended—be ruled admissible. Childers ultimately decided, as he explained in the presence of the jury that day, "that there were things done there that were calculated to scare a man, make him afraid, one of his tribe, by placing the bones of dead white people in his lap, that had been murdered in the community, was calculated to arouse suspicions, things that would make him testify against himself when otherwise he would not," but that enough time had passed between his torment and second confession that it was allowed into evidence. The testimony W.D. Lyons gave when he was called back to the stand was essentially the same as that he'd offered the day before, with one striking difference: county attorney Norman Horton read him his confession line by line, and Lyons disavowed the confession line by line. Horton was playing to the jury with pointed, graphic questions:

"You shot Mr. Rogers, didn't you?"

"And set the house on fire after pouring coal oil on it, didn't you?"

"And let that little four-year-old child burn to death?"

Lyons repeated the phrase "I didn't say that" 128 times.

Now, Belden and Marshall would present their side. It too would be more or less a repeat of the case they'd already made, with two exceptions. Thurgood Marshall intended to double down on his strategy of antagonizing Vernon Cheatwood in order to reveal him to be a liar and unrepentant racist. And the defense had a handful of star witnesses who had not yet testified, who were Lyons's last, and perhaps his best, hope.

"Will you state your name, please?" said Belden.

"Mrs. Vernon Colclasure."

"Mrs. Colclasure, were you related to Mrs. Rogers, Elmer Rogers's wife?"

"Yes sir, I married her brother. Sister-in-law by marriage."

"Do you know Vernon Cheatwood, the governor's special investigator?" Belden asked, calmly. He knew what was coming. This was his witness, after all.

"Yes, I do."

"Do you recall him coming to your home one morning, and there talking to you and to the father of Mrs. Rogers about a confession he had obtained?" Belden said.

"Yes sir."

"What did Mr. Cheatwood do or say, if anything?"

Lattimore, the deputy attorney general, interjected, cutting off the witness before she could respond. "Objected to as incompetent, irrelevant, and immaterial, and calling for hearsay testimony."

Now Marshall stood. "If the court please, yesterday we specifically asked Mr. Cheatwood whether or not he made a statement concerning a blackjack, and he answered that he never made the statement, and I think we are in a position to show that he did."

"And further," Belden added, "he stated at the time that he never had a blackjack."

"I don't know what the law is in New York," Lattimore sneered, "but in Oklahoma in order to impeach you must ask an impeaching question, fixing time and place." His objection was nonsense, but the deputy attorney general was scrambling for something to prevent the truth—that Vernon Cheatwood had bragged openly about using a blackjack to beat W.D. Lyons—from coming out. He was, essentially, stalling for time.

The two sides went back and forth until Marshall and Belden turned to each other and in hushed tones quickly devised a new plan of action.

Belden withdrew the question. This tit for tat wasn't the argument the defense wanted to have. Nor did they need to have it— they simply called Vernon Cheatwood to the stand and Thurgood Marshall eagerly approached the witness.

"On the morning the statement was procured from W.D. Lyons," he said, "do you remember sometime about noon, in the lobby of the Webb Hotel, telling the porter to go upstairs and get your nigger beater?"

"I never made no such statement," Cheatwood snarled.

"Did you have in your hand at any time in the lobby of that hotel a blackjack?" Marshall said.

"I don't remember having a blackjack there in my hand. I don't own one, don't have one."

"Did you, in the presence of the hotel manager, say you beat a confession out of a negro?"

"No."

"Did you, in the presence of Mrs. Vernon Colclasure, say you had beaten a confession out of W.D. Lyons?" Marshall was wholly in his element and enjoying himself. Not only was his prey enthusiastically stumbling into his trap but Marshall was playing another role he relished, that of the black attorney in the South questioning a racist white man who was compelled by law to answer him. The exchange was a singular—and fleeting—reversal of the normal racial power dynamic, and one imagines the scene was heartening, even exhilarating, to many on the black side of the courtroom gallery.

"That morning?" Cheatwood said, squirming.

"Yes sir," Marshall said.

"No, and no other time," Cheatwood said.

"Do you remember talking to Mr. Skeen, the hotel clerk, the man behind the desk, last night, about this case?"

"I don't remember saying anything about it," Cheatwood said. He must have been steaming. "I asked him if he was going to be a witness."

"Did you or did you not suggest that he forget something about his testimony and about what you said?" Marshall said.

"I sure did not."

Marshall excused the witness, and the two defense attorneys must have felt the exhilaration of this moment. They had been like panthers, slowly and methodically pacing and encircling their prey, baiting and prodding, enticing, until the precise right moment to strike, and that moment had finally arrived.

———

"What is your name?" Belden asked his witness.

"Albany Gipson."

"Where were you working on the 23rd of January, 1940?"

"Webb Hotel."

"All right," Belden said. "I will ask you if Mr. Cheatwood, that day, said to you, 'Boy, go up to my room and get me my nigger beater?'"

"Yes sir."

"He did say that?"

"Yes sir."

"What did you do?"

"I went up to his room, and I looked on the dresser, and brought down the thing he called the nigger beater."

"What did you do with it?"

"I brought it downstairs to him."

"Did he make any statement?"

"He said, 'This is what I beat the nigger boy's head with.'"

Belden excused the witness and called another, Leslie Skeen, the bookkeeper at the Webb Hotel, who testified that Cheatwood had asked her for help in finding his blackjack after he misplaced it. In one telling exchange, Skeen's testimony also revealed the behind-the-scenes machinations at work over the course of W.D. Lyons's trial.

"Did Cheatwood, last night, suggest to you that you forget what he said to you in the hotel lobby on the former occasion?" Belden asked.

"Yes," said Skeen, testifying under oath that the state investigator had engaged in witness tampering.

"What did you tell him?" Belden said.

"I told him I hadn't forgotten it and to me it would be telling a lie if I said I had."

Belden excused his witness and called to the stand E. O. Colclasure, the father of Marie Rogers. Colclasure delivered the final blow to the state's case, testifying in pristine detail how one day on a visit to his home after Lyons's arrest Vernon Cheatwood brought out his blackjack to show it off.

"Can you describe it?" Belden asked.

"Well. It was, of course, I guess, one kind of a blackjack. It wasn't one of these long, round ones. It was a machine-stamped red leather, made in the shape of a biscuit, and the handle come up flat."

"Did he in the presence of you and your daughter-in-law say that he had beat the confession out of W.D. Lyons with a blackjack?"

"He pulled the blackjack out of his right coat pocket and bucked his right knee up and whammed it two or three times and said, 'I beat that boy last night for, I think, six—either six or seven hours.' And he said, 'I haven't even got to go to bed last night.'"

———

In his closing statement, county attorney Norman Horton recounted the state's case: that on New Year's Eve a year prior, W.D. Lyons, fueled by whiskey and greed, robbed and brutally murdered Elmer and Marie Rogers and set fire to their home, in the process burning a child alive. "A mad dog has been aloose in this community and the state has caught him," Horton said. "We are asking you to send W.D. Lyons to the electric chair."

Marshall rose to his feet and stepped around the defense table to address the jury.

"I'll agree with just about half the county attorney has said regarding a mad dog being at large in this section, but the only place where I differ with Mr. Horton is in the fact that you haven't caught that mad dog. He's still loose to prey upon you. Killing Lyons will still leave this fiendish brute his freedom to menace your homes."

Next, Belden addressed the jury in a brief statement, laying out the simple fact that, in the balance, the state's case depended entirely on two confessions made under duress. "And when you take out those two confessions, all one has left is a young boy in your community who happened to go rabbit hunting on that unfortunate day when Elmer Rogers was killed and burned. The defense rests."

Now it was time to wait. It was still plenty early for the jury to finish deliberating by the end of the day. Judge Childers excused the jury, the bailiff returned Lyons to a jail cell, and the attorneys filed out of the courtroom to join the teeming mass of people— schoolchildren, reporters, and an assortment of curious locals— who milled around the courthouse waiting for the twelve white men to come to a decision.

A dogged reporter at heart, Dunjee wandered out through the throng to listen to chatter and strike up conversations. Another newspaper reporter approached him for an interview and asked what adjective he preferred. Her newspaper insisted on using the word *Negro*, she said, but "I understand some of you like to be called colored and I would like to know what your people prefer." He deconstructed for her the word *Negro*, explaining that it had no biological or ethnological basis, that she might choose to call him a Zulu or a Bantu, but he wasn't quite sure where in Africa precisely slave traders had kidnapped his ancestors from. Finally he threw a lifeline to the no-doubt bewildered reporter and, perhaps in a nod to his wry reclamation of the word when he gave a name to his own newspaper, he told her she "can use the word 'black' with about the same sense of consistency that the term 'white' is used in talking about people to whose ethnic group you belong."

As he meandered through the crowd, Dunjee was struck yet again by the depth of support there seemed to be for Lyons, even among whites. He heard one white man, whom he later described only as a "hill farmer," puzzling over why Van Bizzell had been let out on bond when the laws were trying to send his supposed accomplice to the electric chair. As Dunjee plugged a coin into a machine to buy a Coca-Cola, a big, hulking farmer with an open shirt collar and mud still caked on his boots approached.

"I know what you're thinking about," the man said. "You're thinking the same thing I'm thinking. That the jury ought to turn that boy free. It's just a put-up job on the part of the penitentiary officials to clear their own folk. They know those convicts were running loose down here and committed that crime and they know they are attempting to send an innocent black boy to the death chair in order to save their own hides."

"We know," Mrs. Colclasure said to Dunjee, "that the attorney told the truth when he said the mad dog had not been caught. None of us believe W.D. Lyons committed that crime and we believe something ought to be done by our county officials to apprehend the guilty parties."

On the street outside the courthouse, Marie Rogers's father, E. O. Colclasure, could hardly contain his contempt for the lawmen he believed were knowingly trying to send an innocent man to death row. "Norman Horton is making the biggest mistake of his life," he told Dunjee. It was the first time in his life, Dunjee later wrote, that he'd seen a trial like this—"in which the majority of white people believe in the innocence of the black man."

After deliberating for five hours the jury reached a verdict, and Judge Childers called court back into session. Lyons sat at a table with his lawyers, attentive as he awaited his fate. The black and white citizens of Choctaw County and beyond packed into the courtroom and listened in breathless silence while the jury foreman read their decision.

"We, the Jury, duly empaneled and sworn in the above entitled cause, do, upon our oaths, find the above named defendant, W.D. Lyons, guilty of murder as charged in the information herein, and fix his punishment at imprisonment in the State Penitentiary for and during his natural life."

Marshall's time in Hugo had stirred something in him. He'd lost the case at the county level, but he had always expected that. Indeed, W.D. Lyons's trial had always been mere prologue—for the NAACP, now the real work began. Now the real plan—the reason they'd taken on Lyons's case from among the thousands of injustices black Americans faced every day—could be launched into action.

After attending meetings with local NAACP groups to raise funds and inspire the faithful in the ongoing fight for civil rights, then a long bus ride back to Oklahoma City and a bit of rest, Marshall took a seat at a desk at the *Black Dispatch* office to hammer out a letter to Walter White back in New York City. He recounted the week's events, reflecting in more detail than in previous letters on Lyons, Hugo, and what the week had meant for the future of the NAACP: "90% of the white people by this time were with Lyons. One thing this trial accomplished—the good citizens of that area have been given a lesson in constitutional law and the rights of Negroes which they won't forget for some time. Law enforcement officers now know that when they beat a Negro up they might have to answer for it on the witness stand."

For the citizens of Choctaw County, black and white, nothing would be the same. "You can't imagine what it means to these people down there who have been pushed around for years to know that there is an organization that will help them. They are really ready to do their part now. They are ready for anything. I think we are in a perfect position to appeal," he wrote to White.

> We will prepare a motion for a new trial and file it Monday the tenth. This case has enough angles to raise a real defense fund over the country if handled properly. I think we should aim at $10,000.* We have already raised around $275 in that small community down there. We can raise more than a thousand in this state. We could use another good defense fund and this case has more appeal than any up to this time. The beating plus the use of the bones of dead people will raise money. I think we should issue a story this week on the start of the defense fund and when I get back on the tenth we can lay plans for a real drive for funds.

It was time now to scale up the battle plan devised ten years earlier in the NAACP's Margold Report to undermine the separate but equal doctrine from within. After struggling to keep the lights

---

* An amount nearly ten times a typical American man's annual earnings in 1941.

on while plodding through essential but less headline-friendly cases on graduate school admissions, voting rights, teacher pay, and the like, Marshall finally had a case that aligned all of his objectives: it advanced case law on vital civil rights policy (in this case the rights of the accused), it came to the aid of a black citizen who had experienced an awful injustice, and, crucially, it promised to rally Americans to the NAACP's cause, make newspaper headlines, and draw desperately needed donations to support the legal front in the long fight against Jim Crow.

"The NAACP did all right this month," Marshall wrote with palpable excitement. "We can raise money on these cases. We have been needing a good criminal case and we have it. Let's raise some real money."

9

"PRESENT BUT NOT subpoenaed," Dunjee said with confidence, suppressing a smile as he heard his name called and rose to his feet amid the overflow crowd of more than a hundred packed into the senate lounge at the Oklahoma state capitol building. Befuddled state senator Joe B. Thompson, presiding over this hearing of the Oklahoma Senate Committee on Privileges and Elections, told Dunjee that he should have received an official summons.

"I did not receive one," Dunjee said. "I'm here only because of what I read in the newspapers." Titters flickered across the crowded room. Senator Thompson struggled to maintain decorum in proceedings that were fast becoming a laughingstock.

It had been only a few days since his return to Oklahoma City from W.D. Lyons's trial in Hugo, but Dunjee was dressed sharply, as always, and eager for the sparring match to come. This was the second week into hearings in Washington of what local press dubbed the "Little Dies Committee"—a nod to Representative Martin Dies, Democrat from Texas and chairman of the Special Committee to Investigate Un-American Activities, precursor to the infamous House Un-American Activities Committee (HUAC) and the McCarthyism of the 1950s—where investigations were under way to root out subversive elements in American society.

By February 1941 war had fully engulfed Europe and Asia. Still in a nonaggression pact with the Soviets, the Nazi Africa Corps under General Rommel was just then rolling across North Africa, racking up victories against the British while Nazi bombers delivered blitzkrieg terror in raids across England. France was firmly under Vichy control. The day Dunjee appeared to testify at the Little Dies Committee, the *Daily Oklahoman* was full of harrowing reports from the European theater—British bombing raids on German positions just across the English Channel; the Greeks repelling, for now, an ongoing Italian offensive; ten thousand Nazis pouring into the Balkans; unconfirmed reports of Generalissimo Francisco Franco, dictator of nominally neutral Spain, meeting secretly with the Vichy French and Italian Fascists. On the home front, the US Army announced the creation of a new air school at the Tuskegee Institute in Alabama, where black Americans would soon, for the first time, train to be military pilots. In the Pacific, Japan maintained its brutal hold over much of China. The empire had struck an alliance with the Axis powers, strengthening the enemies of liberal democracy—though, in a press conference that day, President Roosevelt assured the nation he saw no danger of war between America and Japan.

The United States had so far managed to stay out of the fight, but the country was thrashing in seizures of jingoistic paranoia. Fear of a seditious fifth column lurking unseen in America—closet Nazis or secret Soviets intent on sowing discord, or worse, to weaken the United States—had spread like a fungus across the country. The Dies Committee in Washington was ferreting out subversives at the national level, and, encouraged by Governor Phillips, Oklahoma legislators were determined to root out the Reds they said hid among the state's citizenry awaiting the signal from Moscow to spark a revolution and bring Bolshevism to the streets of Oklahoma City.

Oklahoma officials worried about labor unrest did have some cause for concern. Between 1935 and 1940, after a decade living

under virtually unrelenting economic decline and a taxation system that favored oil companies and big business at the expense
of common consumers, eighty thousand Oklahomans fled the
state (twice as many as the state with the next largest exodus).
One in six Oklahoma farmers was driven off the land, and their
abandoned farms were snapped up by predatory mortgage and
insurance companies and big-money landholders. The state was
thus fertile ground for anyone promising a better deal for the
poor, like the American Communist Party, whose membership
nationally surged to well over fifty thousand by 1940. While Rep.
Martin Dies's committee in Washington investigated the activities
of the pro-Nazi German American Bund and the Communist-
linked American Youth Congress, officials in Oklahoma set to
work cracking down on what Communists they could find in the
lower Great Plains.

The low-hanging fruit in that regard was a group of avowed
Communists who operated the Progressive Bookstore in downtown Oklahoma City where Communist Party meetings were
occasionally held, and which distributed leftist literature, including works like *The Communist Manifesto* and Vladimir Lenin's
The State and Revolution. In August 1940, police had raided the
bookstore and the homes of its operators, arresting patrons and
proprietors alike. The store's owners were charged with criminal
syndicalism (plotting to violently overthrow the government),
and in their trials that commenced that fall they were represented
by a principled and uncompromising member of the American
Civil Liberties Union from Cushing, Oklahoma: Stanley Belden.

As anti-Communist hysteria engulfed Oklahoma, a group of
civic leaders raised the alarm that basic civil rights were being
trampled in the name of ferreting out imagined Bolshevik
bogeymen. With clergy, university professors, and newspaper-
men among their numbers, these concerned citizens formed the

Oklahoma Federation for Constitutional Rights to combat the state's increasingly flagrant infringements on civil liberties. One of the group's original organizers, and a member of its executive committee, was Roscoe Dunjee.

The same economic conditions that made Communism attractive to some poor whites were more acute yet for black Oklahomans. Between 1935 and 1940, one in six farmers in Oklahoma lost their land, but rates of land loss for black farmers, who often had smaller and more precarious farming operations than whites, were even higher. Black Oklahomans faced an unemployment rate twice that of whites. Furthermore, unlike other major political parties in the United States, the Communist Party took an unambiguous and unyielding position in favor of full racial equality.

But Roscoe Dunjee had no affinity for Communist ideology and was adamant that the fact of his consorting with Communists did not make him a Communist. "Following the same line of reasoning," he wrote in one smoldering editorial, "one might aptly decide that all white men are Negroes who occasionally and incidentally chase around with black women at night." His interest, as he editorialized in the *Black Dispatch*, was in preserving civil rights for all. "If a fair trial is denied Communists, if excessive bail is demanded of Communists, and if free speech is denied Communists," Dunjee wrote, "the same rule can be forced upon this writer, his race and all minority groups."

Upon hearing of the creation of the new civil rights federation, Governor Phillips issued a statement to newspapers condemning the group. "This organization about constitutional rights is the height of folly," Phillips said. "No one is denied constitutional rights in Oklahoma." Such a statement made in Jim Crow Oklahoma was preposterous on its face, but in light of what had just transpired in Hugo, Dunjee was particularly incensed. Thus, when he read in the papers that the Little Dies Committee had trained its sights on the Oklahoma Federation for Constitutional Rights and would be issuing subpoenas to bring executive committee members in to testify, he was more than a little eager for the chance to respond. He was not one to shirk from a public war of words, especially with men he referred to scornfully as "gentlemen from the provinces" and "hill-billy patriots." It hardly mattered that through some unknown error—or calculated attempt to portray him as afraid to testify before the committee—Dunjee never actually received his subpoena. He would be there regardless, he said, "with bells on."

The proceedings were already beginning to veer off the rails by the time Dunjee was called to testify on Tuesday, February 11. That morning the committee called up a mathematics professor from the University of Oklahoma, who testified that he was not a Communist but felt it was his duty "as a citizen to help or defend civil rights in this state." Senator Thompson, who could claim only an elementary school education, demanded the professor produce copies of his published work to inspect for subversive content. "This stuff may be mathematics," said a confounded Thompson, scanning through papers on subjects like integral calculus, "but it doesn't look like anything I ever studied." An observer said later he overheard one legislator mutter something about "Communist code."

When Dunjee took the stand, Thompson asked him what was discussed at the first meeting of the federation he attended. "The first item on our program related to the denial of civil rights to a Negro down in Choctaw County," Dunjee replied. "His name is W.D. Lyons."

He continued: "We tried that case in Hugo, Oklahoma, last week and the evidence showed that a special investigator of Governor Phillips, Vernie Cheatwood, together with two highway patrolmen, had through force and violence, extorted a confession from W.D. Lyons. I think this case shows concrete evidence of the denial of civil rights in Oklahoma."

"Well," Thompson retorted, "your civil rights group did not develop its program solely on Negro issues, did it?"

"No sir," said Dunjee, "not by any means. I am just beginning to tell you about the remainder of our program. Shall I proceed?"

State senator Paul Stewart—from the town of Antlers, twenty miles north of Hugo—blurted out a response: "No, we don't want to know any more about your program."

At that, the crowd cracked up into chuckles. The absurdity of a state senator commanding a witness not to respond to a question he had just been asked was too much to bear. Senator Thompson tried to steer the discussion back on course.

"Are you a communist?" he asked.

"No," said Dunjee.

"Do you know any communists?"

"Yes."

"Who?"

"Oh, I know Robert Wood, his wife, Eli Jaffe, Alan Shaw," Dunjee said, listing the names of those who had recently been on very public trial for their open and unapologetic membership in the Communist Party. "Oh, it would be impossible for me to tell you all the communists I know."

Laughter bubbled over in the audience again—Dunjee was making a mockery of the hearings, and having a ball. Thompson continued trying to pin him down, but Dunjee wouldn't be forced into a yes or no answer, allowing only that he was "opposed to the economic theories of Communists."

"I positively oppose them," he said. "I have a little business and I—"

"Well," interjected Stewart again, "we do not want any oratory."

"We'll just remove the Negro question from this discussion," Thompson said, in a stunning admission from a state legislator. "You know there is in this country a Negro problem and always will be. Aside from the denial of rights to Negroes, what other denials of civil rights can you recall?"

"Of course you know," said Dunjee, "I do not agree that there will always be a Negro problem. You should also keep in mind that whatever affects the Negro has a similar bad effect upon white people. I mean this in the sense that no man can hold another man in the ditch without being down in the ditch with the man he holds."

Unsatisfied with where his own line of questioning was headed, Thompson pivoted to a different tactic in his effort to trip Dunjee up. "Well, you're a member of a civil rights group. Can you tell this committee anything about the Bill of Rights?"

"That's a good question," Dunjee said. He proceeded to describe the various limits on government overreach enumerated in the first ten amendments to the US Constitution. "I don't know whether I can tell you all that's in the Bill of Rights," he said in closing. "I know, however, that as a Negro, I'm not getting any civil rights."

Cheers and applause thundered across the gallery. Stewart stopped the proceedings and singled out one of those who had cheered. "What's your name?" he demanded.

"I haven't been subpoenaed," said the young man, Duane Spradling, a student at the University of Oklahoma.

"You just think you haven't," Stewart fumed. He ordered half a dozen of those who had applauded, including Spradling, out of the room to be sworn in as witnesses and subpoenaed to appear before the committee the next day.

Three other members of the Oklahoma Federation for Constitutional Rights were called before the committee before it adjourned for the day, including University of Oklahoma religion professor Nick Comfort. When asked to cite examples of constitutional rights violations in Oklahoma, Comfort listed several. First among them was the beating of W.D. Lyons at the hands of law enforcement authorities in Hugo.

Stewart angrily interrupted his witness again. "Do you sympathize with communist ideas?" he barked.

"No," Comfort said, "probably not half as much as you do Senator."

Stewart asked what he thought of the public display of red flags.

"It depends on what you mean," Comfort said. "It depends on what the flags mean. I was out in western Oklahoma the other day and saw hundreds of red flags waving in the fields and I was about to call Governor Phillips' attention to it when I discovered they were surveyors' flags." More laughter from the crowd. Stewart demanded a straight answer "without the comedy." Did Comfort approve of displaying red flags in parades?

"Take the case of the Rotary Club," Comfort replied, "which uses all the flags of the nations. Now if I saw a parade by the Rotary Club and the flags of all the other nations were in the parade I think it would be all right for them to have a red flag for Russia, too."

Last to appear before the committee that day was the Reverend Paul Wright, former cochairman of the foundation. Asked to give his definition of a Communist, Wright said he'd offer the same definition he gave a high school girl who once asked him the same question.

"He is one who believes in dialectical materialism," Wright said.

The stenographer stopped. "Dia— what?"

"You mean that's the definition you gave that high school girl?" Stewart asked.

"Yes," Wright said, according to a report of the proceedings in the *Daily Oklahoman*, "and what's more she was intelligent enough to understand it."

Laughter roared and echoed in the crowded senate lounge and Thompson rapped for order.

When the hearing picked back up the following morning the circus atmosphere reached a crescendo. J. W. Reed, Grand Dragon of the Ku Klux Klan in Oklahoma, sat in the audience, where he announced the Klan's support for the hearings. He also distributed an expansive pamphlet that extolled the virtues of the Little Dies Committee, lambasted the Oklahoma Federation for Constitutional Rights as dupes if not foreign agents, promised the Klan's backing in the fight against "the enemies within our gates—the radical pacifists, the criminals, the pinks, the reds, the yellows as well as the Fascist and Nazi groups of the extreme right," and made liberal use of all capital letters throughout.

In a flurry of activity, committee members fearful of being associated with the KKK ordered building employees to gather up and dispose of all copies of the pamphlet that Reed had scattered around the capitol. Amid the ruckus, Dunjee found and held onto a copy of the pamphlet. If he feared the consequences of giving the Klan a platform to spread its message of racist hate, he didn't show it. Intent on continuing to ridicule the Little Dies Committee by exposing the racist right-wing hysteria of some who supported its work, Dunjee reprinted the KKK pamphlet in full in the next issue of the *Black Dispatch*.*

---

* Four defendants in the Progressive Bookstore raids were ultimately convicted and imprisoned on charges of criminal syndicalism. Their charges were overturned by the Oklahoma Court of Criminal Appeals, and charges against all other parties involved were dropped. Oklahoma's Little Dies Committee continued its work for several months and on May 7, 1941, with patriotic fervor in America roiling, issued a report claiming there was a well-financed cadre of one thousand Communist Party members in Oklahoma that functioned as a "propaganda agency for the Soviet Union of Russia." The report recommended a bill banning

———————

Fireworks at the Little Dies hearing petered out in the weeks that followed, but those early, lively days of the hearings made at least one thing abundantly clear: for people in Oklahoma who were concerned about upholding civil liberties and basic constitutional rights, the case of W.D. Lyons was on their minds.

For Roscoe Dunjee these were especially troubling times. Not only was he embroiled in a red scare in Oklahoma City but due to his involvement in the Oklahoma Federation for Constitutional Rights, officials at Langston University, his alma mater, canceled a speech he'd been scheduled to deliver. On top of that, his sister, Drusilla Dunjee Houston—herself a contributor to the *Black Dispatch* and an accomplished historian—passed away that week.

Then there was the Lyons matter. On Tuesday at the state capitol building, Dunjee ran into Stanley Belden, who informed him that he'd filed an appeal on Lyons's behalf as planned the day before, but that the court clerk told him the cost of preparing the case made (the document necessary for Lyons's appeal) would run about $250—a tidy sum for the scrappy civil rights organization. Additionally, for reasons lost to history, Van Bizzell—out on bond and rumored to have been told to leave Choctaw County and never return—was arrested in Tulsa and brought back to Hugo.

———————

Communist Party members from holding elective office in Oklahoma (a measure the legislature passed by a huge majority the next day), as well as terminating the employment of University of Oklahoma language professor Dr. Maurice Halperin. The university complied, but soon offered to reinstate him, an offer Halperin declined. Halperin later went to work for the US military's Office of Strategic Services, the precursor to the Central Intelligence Agency. In 1948, confessed Soviet agent and Communist defector Elizabeth Bentley named Halperin as a spy for the Soviet Union during his time at the OSS.

Dunjee was in need of a morale boost when he wrote to Marshall on February 13, 1941, "I told you I was the best witness South of hell or North of Texas," encouraging Marshall to read what the papers "had to say this evening about your humble servant."

Left to right: Ray Harmon, sheriff; R. L. Gee, assistant county attorney; Reasor Cain, Frisco special agent; Floyd Brown, deputy sheriff; W.D. Lyons; Howard Rorie, constable; and Vernon Cheatwood, special investigator for the governor. *Library of Congress NAACP Archive*

During his travels, Thurgood Marshall sometimes wrote detailed letters to his colleagues back in New York, like this letter, scribbled out in a hurry early on in the trial. *Author photo*

Leon C. "Red" Phillips was a staunch anti–New Deal Democrat. His administration was fraught with accusations of corruption. *Library of Congress Harris & Ewing photograph collection*

37093

Name: W. D. Lyons
Entered: 1-4-38   County: Choctaw
Crime: Larceny of domestic fowls
Sentence: 3 years   Costs: $10.95
Maximum: 1-3-41.   Minimum: 10-4-39
10-27-39

Wanted by:

1-8-38 Neg.
Residence: Hugo, Okla.

Prior Convictions: O.S.P. 22701

OCT 27 1939

Age: 19 (1938) Color: Negro
Eyes: Brown   Hair: Brown
Wt: 170   Ht: 6-1
Comp. Brown   Bld: Slender

F. P. C. 12 M I H 00I 12
M I H 00C 10

W.D. Lyons's ID card from the short stint he did in prison for stealing chickens. Lyons had been out of prison only a couple months when he was arrested for the Rogers family murder. *Author photo*

Founder and editor of the *Black Dispatch* and a close friend of Thurgood Marshall, Roscoe Dunjee was a prominent African American civic leader in Oklahoma for several decades. Here he delivers a speech during a parade in Oklahoma City in 1942. *Oklahoma Historical Society*

A brilliant jurist, Thurgood Marshall was also an animated trial lawyer with a knack for courtroom theatrics, skills he put to good use while defending W.D. Lyons. *Library of Congress NAACP Archive*

Stanley Belden—W.D. Lyons's first attorney and Oklahoma's representative of the American Civil Liberties Union—had a well-earned reputation as a stern and principled fighter for civil rights in Oklahoma. *David Belden*

The Choctaw County courthouse in Hugo, Oklahoma. *Oklahoma Historical Society*

The Oklahoma State Penitentiary, near McAlester. *Oklahoma Historical Society*

Prisoners and guards alike referred to the electric chair in the Oklahoma State Penitentiary as "Old Sparky." After beating him, guards left W.D. Lyons to spend a while in the room with Old Sparky—an unsubtle message to say the least. *Oklahoma Historical Society*

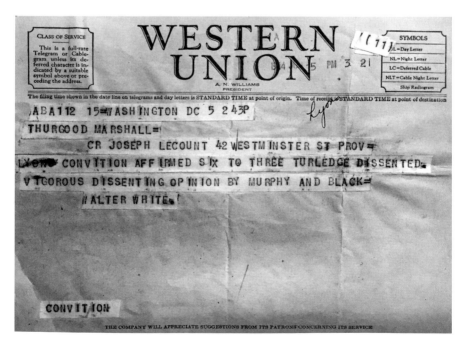

In this letter, W.D. Lyons's mother pleads with the NAACP to help her son. *Author photo*

Much of the communication between the interested parties in the Lyons matter—spread out as they were across the country—took place via telegrams like this one. This telegram from Walter White to Thurgood Marshall is how Marshall first learned that he had lost the Lyons case in the Supreme Court. *Author photo*

A poor farmhand and petty criminal, W.D. Lyons was just twenty-one years old when he was arrested. *Library of Congress NAACP Archive*

W.D. Lyons in handcuffs standing behind the shotgun the authorities said he used to kill the Rogers family. *Library of Congress NAACP Archive*

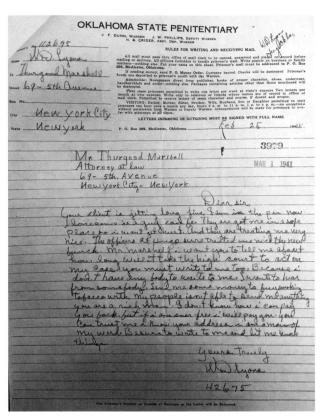

The changes in W.D. Lyons's letters over the years reflected a man with little education studying diligently to improve his lot. In this letter, the first he wrote to Marshall from prison, some of his characters are written backward. It is possible another prisoner helped him with this one by taking dictation and writing for him. *Author photo*

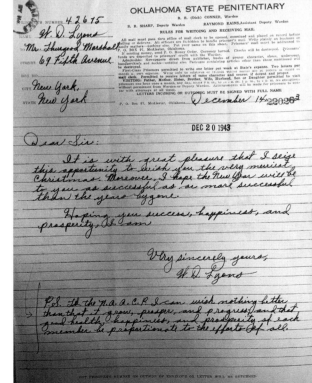

In this letter, written in late December 1943, Lyons shows off his dramatically improved handwriting and command of written English to wish Marshall "the very merriest Christmas." *Author photo*

10

THE FOLLOWING TWO CHAPTERS *are composed largely of a careful selection of letters between the key people involved in the Lyons case. The authors' intent in faithfully reproducing these letters is to evoke the spirit of the times and allow the personalities of each man to subtly emerge as the story unfolds one piece of correspondence at a time.*

Thurgood Marshall to Roscoe Dunjee
February 14, 1941
Dear Dunjee,

Sorry I have not had a chance to write you sooner, but on my return to the office I found my desk loaded with cases and other matters. I have not finished them yet. I have just received your letter and the newspaper clippings concerning your testimony before the "Little Dies" committee. Some people get all the breaks!

Needless to say, I knew you would spank the boys. I have passed the clippings around to the rest of the fellows in the office and they all join me in the realization that you did a splendid job.

At the meeting of the American Civil Liberties Union last Monday I placed before them the entire question of the denial of Civil Liberties in the State of Oklahoma.

I am more than happy that I came out for the Lyons case and the meeting with the teachers. We are laying plans for the raising of the Defense Fund and a large part of the bulletin to our branch members for this month will be devoted to the Lyons case as the opening gun in our drive for funds. I will keep you advised of all developments and look forward to seeing you very soon.

　　　　　　　　　With best wishes, I remain, Sincerely yours,

　　　　　　　　　　　　　　　Thurgood Marshall

PS: I trust that Iowa* has fully recovered and that he has learned his lesson and will not be caught again in the position of standing still when he should have been running.

Stanley Belden to Thurgood Marshall
February 14, 1941
Dear Friend Marshall,

I went to Hugo last Sunday and obtained some more evidence in the Lyons case. I have a witness now who is willing to swear that Van Ralston told him that he beat Lyons at the penitentiary before they got the confession.

I argued the motion and read a number of cases but the court overruled our motion for a new trial as we expected he would.

I am enclosing a letter from the reporter. The casemade is costing more than I expected it would, but there is nothing we can do about it except pay it. I had him cut out the voir dire examination and argument of counsel. The extra copy will cost twenty-five dollars ($25.00) which will make a total of two hundred seventy-five dollars ($275.00) and the reporter wants a part of it immediately.

---

* Dunjee's famously overweight bulldog.

This case is receiving considerable comment through the state and the people in Hugo in general want to see this case reversed.

As soon as the casemade is prepared, one copy will be sent to you immediately. The next thing, of course, will be a Petition in Error.

I will get the casemade to you at the earliest possible date.

I talked to Dunjee yesterday in Oklahoma City at the "Red" hearing. Dunjee in particular, and the rest of the witnesses in general certainly took care of themselves on the stand. The Senate Committee got rid of Dunjee as though he were too hot to handle. They denied him rights in that they demanded him to answer questions "yes" or "no" and then would not permit him to explain. Even at that he certainly took care of himself, and the Oklahoma Federation for Constitutional Rights is stronger than ever. They will appear there before the Committee again next Tuesday. I will be there in attendance, of course. I have not been subpoenaed yet but I expect to be. They bandied my name about during the hearing last Tuesday. The committee tried to discredit me when one witness, Dr. Comfort, Dean of Religion, stated that the information as to the Lyons case was obtained from me. One of the Senators then spoke up and said "Belden spent a year behind bars, didn't he?" The Committee members are special friends of the governor and the governor has been catching hell in this Lyons case and naturally, he is trying to get back at me.

I have received a letter from Roger Baldwin stating that you gave a very vivid report of affairs in Oklahoma and I am sure that you did. He spoke of my sending them an affidavit as to conditions here. I think immediately at the close of this red hearing that it should be done. So far, the "red" hearing has been a boomerang to the Senators all witnesses having taken care of themselves in such a very fine manner that the papers reported it in such a way as to reflect upon the Senate Committee.

Sincerely yours,

Stanley Belden

Thurgood Marshall to Roscoe Dunjee

February 17, 1941

Dear Dunjee,

I have just received a long letter from Stanley Belden giving all the details concerning the appeal in the Lyons case. It seems that he needs $275.00 to have the transcript of the record typed by the Court Stenographer and he must have a part of it immediately.

We do not have any funds in the office now and I am wondering if you can have Bullock send the part payment out of the money on hand so that there will be no delay in the appeal.

Sincerely yours,

Thurgood Marshall

Special Counsel

Roscoe Dunjee to Thurgood Marshall

February 19, 1941

My dear Thurgood,

Have just read your letter regarding the transcript at Hugo. Belden talked to me about this matter twice but in each instance he said the clerk said the approximate cost would be $250.00.

I have just written to Dr. Williamston telling him to go to Hugo and personally assure the clerk he may proceed with the work and that he will be paid. I am also sending a circular letter out to the branches today asking them to raise money to take care of this particular cost.

I am of the opinion that we ought to care for these costs through Williamston instead of Belden. My experience with Chandler teaches me that we can keep out chisling by handling the matter direct. I am of the opinion that it will be best to handle all of the matters from the national office through my office or something may go wrong. You can see the costs raised $25.00 when Belden wrote you.

At any rate I do not anticipate any trouble in raising the cost of the transcript here. You perhaps caused Belden to get excited when you told him we would raise a National Defense Fund. He was telling me yesterday he had fig-ured up driving 4000 miles since the case started. This is a physical impossibility, since I know how many times he has been to Hugo and one trip to McAlester. This is indicatory of his beginning to see things.

Give my regards to the boys in the office. My little "Dies" outfit are about to go in their hole and pull the hold in behind them.

Sincerely,

Roscoe Dunjee

Thurgood Marshall to Roscoe Dunjee
February 20, 1941
Dear Roscoe,
Thanks for your letter of February 19. I agree with you fully concerning Dr. Williamston's handling the costs of the record in the Lyons case.

Please tell Williamston that he is supposed to send us his suggestions concerning the raising of a large defense fund in other states. We had better get started on this as soon as possible. I will be in Texas from March 5 to 12 and hope that I will be able to stop in Oklahoma City, although I doubt it very much because it will be a rush trip.

Best regards to everyone.

Sincerely yours,
Thurgood Marshall
Special Counsel

In February 1941, jazzman Duke Ellington laid down the signature recording of his ode to Harlem, "Take the A Train." Heavyweight boxing champion Joe Louis appeared unstoppable as he knocked out one opponent after the next, still at the beginning of what would be the longest-ever reign of a heavyweight champion. On Broadway, rehearsals were under way for the dramatic adaptation of Richard Wright's novel *Native Son*. While President Franklin Delano Roosevelt still endeavored to keep the United States out of the global conflict now aflame from East Asia to North Africa to Western Europe, the American economy was already mobilizing for the war effort—defense industries were hiring new workers by the thousands, and black civic leaders began demanding equal access to those jobs for African Americans. But for W.D. Lyons, life inside the thick, towering, enamel-white prison walls at the Oklahoma State Penitentiary was not so exciting.

For a year prior, Lyons had been living at the jail in Hugo, and he'd been more or less comfortable there. The jailers involved in his arrest and beating had been thrown out in the most recent elections, and the new lot had made life easier for him. Now a convict with a life sentence, he'd been transferred to the state prison in McAlester—an institution still under the authority of Warden Jess Dunn.

The prison population of around 3,250 was segregated by race, black prisoners in one cellblock, and white and Native American prisoners in another, but Lyons was segregated from the general population further still, ostensibly—and perhaps legitimately— for his protection. While the rest of the population rose early to head out on work crews—to the prison's brickyard, where they fashioned the materials the prisoners themselves used to repair buildings and construct new ones, or to the two-thousand-acre farm that supplied almost all of the prison's food—Lyons was at first restricted to his cell, with perhaps a little time alone in an outdoor recreation area. He could check books and newspapers out of the prison library. Once per week he was allowed to write a letter to someone on a preapproved list of close relatives and friends. But in 1941, W.D. Lyons was only marginally literate, the labored script of his handwritten letters reflective of a person for whom writing even a simple note took great focus. His family was miles away now, and even the small price of postage would have been a noticeable bite out of what little money they had. Lyons spent long hours during those first months in prison alone in a cell with little more than his thoughts.

W.D. Lyons to Thurgood Marshall
February 25, 1941
Dear sir,
Your client is getting long fine. I am in the pen now lonesome as a guy can be. They are got me in a safe place so I won't get hurt. And they are treating me very nice. The officers at Hugo sure treated me nice the new bunch. Mr. Marshall I want you to tell me about how long will it take the high court to act on my case. You must write

to me too. Because I don't have anybody to write to me. I want to hear from somebody. Send me some money to buy smoking tobacco with. My people isn't able to send me anything. You are a nice man. I don't know how I can pay you back. But if I am ever free I will pay you you can trust me I know your address I am a man of my word. Be sure to write to me and let me know things.

Yours truely,
W.D. Lyons

Secretary of Thurgood Marshall to W.D. Lyons
March 17, 1941
Dear Mr. Lyons,

In Mr. Marshall's absence I wish to acknowledge your letter of February 25th. I will call it to his attention on his return to the office. We are happy to learn that you are getting along fine. Keep us advised on how you are from time to time. When Mr. Marshall returns to the office he will write you.

Sincerely yours,
Secretary to Thurgood Marshal
Special Counsel

Memorandum to Oklahoma Branches from NAACP
National Office
March 17, 1941
Two hundred and fifty ($250.00) dollars is immediately necessary for the transcription of the record in the W.D. Lyons case, with which case you must certainly be familiar through the medium of the Bulletin and press releases of the Association.

The Branches in southeastern Oklahoma raised $322.00 while the case was being tried six weeks ago. The appeal was filed in Hugo ten days later and the clerk of the court has advised that the cost of transcribing the testimony at the trial will approximate $250.00.

This case has received national attention. All during the recent "Little Dies Committee" hearing held at the Oklahoma State Capitol and in which Roscoe Dunjee, president of the Oklahoma State Conference of the N.A.A.C.P. Branches participated, white members of the Oklahoma Federation for Constitutional Rights referred to the Lyons case as a positive denial of civil rights. In addition a nationally known magazine is preparing to run an article dealing with the forced confession extorted from this young Negro.

If we are to cement the gains won during 1940 by virtue of our five victories in the United States Supreme Court and numerous others, we must rally to this case and the others now pending in the United States Supreme Court and in state courts.

Our legal defense fund has been depleted by the Spell case and others. To cover immediate future expenditures we need $5000.

Certainly these important steps in the establishment of full citizenship rights for Negro Americans is a product worth selling and at such a price we trust your community will subscribe at least twice its quota. As soon as possible, please send your contribution to Dr. W.A. J. Bullock, Treasurer, 917 South First Street, Chickasha, Okla.

LET'S GO! WHILE BUILDING A FUND FOR NATIONAL DEFENSE, WE MUST BUILD A FUND FOR RACE DEFENSE!

Yours for more and greater victories,
Thurgood Marshall
Special Counsel

Thurgood Marshall to Roy Wilkins, editor of the Crisis *and former assistant to Walter White*
March 31, 1941
Please note the attached letter from W.D. LYONS, OKLA-HOMA, in which he requests a little spending money for smoking tobacco and other items. I am wondering about the possibility of sending him three or four dollars to be deposited with the Warden for his use. This check should be drawn against the INC. FUND.

The members of his family have already contributed all the money they have to the Oklahoma Defense Fund.

Stanley Belden to Thurgood Marshall
March 31, 1941
Dear Friend Marshall:
I talked to Mr. Dunjee last Friday. Altogether there has been seven people called him over the phone from the State Capitol Building about the Lyons case. When the first one called him I told Mr. Dunjee that I thought that if we played our hand right we would find that the Governor was back of the calls, and the last one was an investigator out of the Governor's office.

They proposed that we have the case dismissed on the grounds that the Judge was out of the county while the jury was deliberating (that is ground for dismissal in this state) but I am not sure that the Judge was out of the county while the jury was deliberating, but whether he was or not they gave Mr. Dunjee to understand that they would have Lyons released on this ground, but they told Mr. Dunjee that he would have to get rid of Belden.

They told Mr. Dunjee they were doing this because of their friendship for him but ended up saying it would cost about twenty-five hundred dollars for a guarantee of the release of Lyons. Finally asked Mr. Dunjee what he would pay to get Lyons free.

Now I feel certain that the Governor doesn't want this case appealed to the Criminal Court of Appeals and all the facts be placed before the public. It is one thing to have it published in the papers but a far different thing to have it before the people of the state in a court decision. The Governor has further political ambitions and this case is causing him great embarrassment and if it could be disposed of on the technicality of the Judge being out of the county during the deliberation of the jury, he would be saved politically.

Recently three measures sponsored by the Governor were submitted to the people and they carried in every county of the State with the exception of Choctaw county where the Lyons case was tried.

Now, I am fully aware of our duty to our client but I am also aware of our duty to expose and not cover up the things that make possible such travesty on justice as took place in the Lyons case, and I feel it our duty to the colored race, to the state and all concerned that we file the appeal and expose the corruption in this state even though in so doing to some degree we risk the liberty of our client and make sure that for some months to come he must stay in prison: but after all this thing is bigger than just the question of the immediate liberty of W.D. Lyons or any other individual.

Please let me hear from you by return mail.

Stanley D. Belden

11

THURGOOD MARSHALL WAS in Texas when the national NAACP office received the March 31 letter from Stanley Belden. The work he was doing there helps explain what happened next.

In the early 1940s, with a sharp drop in lynchings across the United States and black Americans migrating en masse from the rural South to the cities where wartime industrialization was creating new employment opportunities, the focus of the NAACP's activities turned increasingly to fighting Jim Crow on the legal front. Marshall's legal department—sometimes called the Inc. Fund—was, by 1941, a separate entity for fundraising purposes. As a separate and ostensibly apolitical entity, donations to the Inc. Fund were tax deductible, but the office had to stand on its own—the handful of lawyers working out of New York under Marshall's leadership could no longer (as an official matter at least) draw on the NAACP's membership dues to fund their many courthouse battles across the country.

And they were busy. Pursuing their strategy of undermining the separate but equal doctrine by forcing the states to actually live up to its impossible promise, the Inc. Fund was bringing lawsuits at a ferocious pace: forcing states to pay black teachers salaries equal to those for whites and suing to force states to either allow black students into professional schools or create schools for black students that were truly equal in every respect.

Through its criminal defense work such as the *Spell* case in Connecticut and the *Lyons* case in Oklahoma, the office pursued another strategy: fighting for the rights of black Americans inside the criminal justice system, which had long been one of the most effective tools for perpetuating white supremacy. The Inc. Fund pursued yet another strategy in Texas, where Marshall sued to end so-called white primaries, whereby blacks were effectively barred from participating in politics by being excluded from voting in Democratic primaries in states dominated entirely by the Democratic Party. As with the other cases the organization took on, the Texas primary case was important not simply in order to seek justice for one person who hadn't been allowed to vote, or even to end the white primary system in all of Texas. The purpose of taking on the case was to establish legal precedent that would make white primaries illegal throughout the country and thus, through clever means, make political power available to black Americans at a time when legislation as sweeping as the Voting Rights Act of 1965 was an impossibility.

Running this multifaceted legal campaign required money. In addition to Marshall's meager salary of $2,600 per year (roughly half the average lawyer's salary in all of America, not to speak of New York City, in 1941), there were salaries for the other attorneys and the secretaries. Also, Marshall traveled tens of thousands of miles a year working on cases all over the country. By staying with local families he saved money on hotels (which weren't typically open to him anyway, or to any African Americans, in the regions he frequented), but there were train fares and bus tickets and gasoline for the car to consider—plus operating expenses such as office supplies, telegrams, and postage, and essential but laborious tasks like making copies in an age before the photocopier. Even keeping a close eye on expenses, costs added up, which is why fundraising for the new legal defense fund was absolutely essential to the success of the NAACP's all-important campaign to destroy the legal foundations of white supremacy. For the cash-strapped new legal defense fund, taking cases that not only won justice for its clients and advanced legal precedent but also drew the attention of the public and inspired donations was a matter of survival.

And the *Lyons* case was a winner. Though they had lost in Hugo, Marshall and Belden were meticulous about putting objections into the record of the trial that would form the basis of their appeal. The state had admitted, on the record, that Lyons had been beaten before making his purported confession. With Marshall's recent success in the *Chambers* case, in which the Supreme Court overturned the confessions of defendants secured through coercion, Lyons's prospects in an appellate court—if not the Oklahoma Criminal Court of Appeals then surely the Supreme Court of the United States—looked very promising indeed.

Meanwhile, publicity about Lyons's ordeal was beginning to inspire exactly the upwelling of support for civil rights work that the NAACP had hoped it would. SOUTHEASTERN OKLAHOMA AFLAME FOR LYONS DEFENSE FUND, read one headline across the top of an entire page of a March 1941 issue of the *Black Dispatch*. The articles beneath described a swelling of membership and outpouring of donations in the small communities of Little Dixie. Even E. O. Colclasure, Marie Rogers's father, had joined the NAACP to support Lyons's defense. And this was before the NAACP had put the Lyons case front and center in a national drive for funds.

Belden's letter describing the offer made by unnamed authorities in Oklahoma to drop charges against Lyons was deemed important enough by the national office that a copy was made and forwarded to Marshall while he was in Houston. Marshall wrote immediately to Belden in response. Though the letter has been lost to history, upon Marshall's return to the office in New York he described its contents in a hastily handwritten note: "Wrote Belden 4-6-41 telling him to file the appeal—no compromise—"

There's no way around the problematic nature of the decision—on which Marshall and Belden were apparently in agreement—not to pursue the opening for Lyons's immediate release. In Belden's telling, the various offers made by state authorities may have hinted at bribery, but on that point the corrupt authorities were apparently willing to negotiate. The offer, as presented, would have involved making the almost certainly false claim that Judge Childers was not in Choctaw County for the five hours the jury was deliberating, but there is no evidence that any of W.D. Lyons's attorneys explored this or some other less unseemly avenue for the state authorities to save face while Lyons walked free. Most troublingly, there is no evidence that anyone ever discussed the offer with W.D. Lyons.

———————

Secretary of Thurgood Marshall to W.D. Lyons
April 10, 1941
Dear Mr. Lyons:
Mr. Thurgood Marshall was in the office for just a short while but had to leave for another state where he is working on a case. However, your letter was called to his attention and he was glad to hear that you are getting along well.

We have sent in care of the Warden a Money Order for Three Dollars to be deposited to your account for smoking tobacco and other small items. As you know, this Association exists through voluntary contributions and our budget is very limited. All our funds must be used to fight for Negroes throughout the country and we can rarely afford to contribute even a small amount for other items. However we are sending you this small amount with great pleasure.

Of course, the attorneys are working on your case. Please continue to keep us advised on how you are and we know you will keep your chin up.

SINCERELY,
Secretary to THURGOOD MARSHALL

W.D. Lyons to Thurgood Marshall
April 21, 1941
Dear Mr. Marshall,

I received the letter that your secretary wrote and i want to let you know that i was very happy to hear from you all. I got the money that you sent me, it reach me in just the right time. I certainly appreciated the loan. Mr Marshall if i ever get a chance, i will send it back to you.

I am getting along fine in health but not in mind. If i ever get a new a new trial I will be lucky it is some things that i would like to tell you, but i can't now. I will tell you if i will be lucky enough to see you again.

Well Mr. Marshall you must write to me all along. I likes to hear from you all, and others too. I am still going to school trying to get me an education, because i wants to be a business man someday. In six months time, i will finish high school.

Mr. Marshall i read about you in the paper, I hope you will be successful in winning that case in Houston Texas. I read about Mr. Dunjee and Mr. Williamson* too. They are very fine men, and you are a swell guy your self. I don't have much to say, so remember and write to me.

Yours Respectfully,
W.D. Lyons

---

* A civic leader and regional NAACP leader based in Idabel, Oklahoma.

Mr Marshall send me a picture of your self when you write again.

Stanley Belden to Thurgood Marshall
April 26, 1941
Dear friend Marshall:
I hope this finds all going well with you.

I am still feeling the repercussion from the Lyons case.

I have just received a letter from the court reporter and he has completed the case made and I will send a copy to New York, immediately, if that is where you want it sent.

I expect to leave here for the West within the next two weeks. My practice here has been ruined because of the various cases involving Civil Rights that I have participated in.

As I understood you, you would have the New York office to prepare a brief in the Lyons case and I would go over the brief before we file and when the case is ready to be argued I will come back for the argument.

I hate very much to leave here and start a new in a different state but the Governor has such a hold on this state that he can and is seeing that my practice is destroyed. I will leave here broke, but have no regrets for doing what I believe is my duty. My only ambition is to get on my feet so I can battle for those things that I believe in in the near future.

With kindest personal regards,
Stanley D. Belden

Thurgood Marshall to Stanley Belden
April 29, 1941
Dear Mr. Belden:
What is the present status of the Lyons case? Do you have a copy of the transcript yet? Please let me know how much time we have left to perfect the appeal and what further

steps are necessary. As soon as we receive a copy of the transcript we will be ready to start on the brief. I think that we can take most of the responsibility for this which will lighten your burden.

With best wishes to you and your Secretary, I remain,

Sincerely,

Thurgood Marshal

Special Counsel

Stanley Belden to Thurgood Marshall
May 6, 1941

Dear Mr. Marshall,

I am, today, sending you a copy of the case-made in the Lyon's case. I will appreciate your office taking most of the responsibility for getting out the brief; as I am leaving here for the West coast within a few days.

As I told you sometime ago, my participation in various Civil Liberties cases, including the Lyons's case, has resulted in the ruining of my practice and since the Governor of this state now has such an iron-grip on it through his appointment of the Industrial Commission, I find I cannot win a case before the Industrial Commission.

The Lyons's case will not be reached by the Criminal Court of Appeals before next September or October so Judge Barefoot, presiding judge of the Criminal Court of Appeals, told me last week. I will arrange to come back to argue the case then.

The special investigator for the Attorney General's Office told an Oklahoma City Attorney, who is a friend of mine, that if I would file a motion to dismiss the Lyons's case by reason of Judge Childers having been out of the county during the deliberation of the jury that the case would be dismissed and that within two weeks they would arrest the two white men that committed the murder. They say they know who they are, that they are bootleggers and that the murder of Roger's was a result of their quarrels over bootlegging and the division of profit; this certainly is a very queer situation if the authorities know they committed the murder, and they stated positively that they do, it certainly is the duty of the authorities to arrest, immediately, and prosecute the murderers and not let murderers run loose. Why should the arrest be contingent on the dismissal of the Lyons's case if it is not a political move to prevent an appeal to be filed in the Lyons's case and the public learn the truth, which certainly would affect the Governor's political ambitions. This is the first time they ever suggested that I go ahead with the dismissal; before they had always told Mr. Dunjee that they must get rid of Belden before anything could be done.

We have until the tenth day of July to file our brief and we can get an extension of time of thirty days then if necessary, but I suggest the filing of the brief in the near future.

I have taken care of having the case-made signed by the County Attorney, Judge Childers, and Court Clerk as provided for by law.

The filing of a petition in error is the next step and if you will prepare it and send it down I will have it filed by an attorney here who is taking care of other matters for me or I will prepare it myself and have it filed if you want me to do this.

My secretary is no longer with me as I am leaving here, but I will remember you to her when I see her when I go West.

With kindest personal regards,

Stanley D. Belden

Thurgood Marshall to Stanley Belden
May 7, 1941
Dear Friend Belden:
Your letter of April 26 has been forwarded to me in New York. If you will send me the record in the case I will get to work on it immediately and start work on the brief. Please let me know exactly how much time we have left for filing the appeal. We will be able to take over full responsibility for the brief but will only send you the drafts for your suggestions. The main idea is to take as much of the responsibility for the work off you but at the same time to have you continue in the case. Please bear in mind that regardless of where you go we simply must have you back for the argument on this case because I am positive we would be unable to get along without this assistance.

I am more than sorry to learn that you are leaving the State but after our several talks on the matter I understand your position and certainly agree with your decision. There is no doubt in my mind that one of these days the officials of our States will begin to realize the true meaning of Civil Liberties but at least you can be satisfied with the feeling that you have made your contribution.

With best wishes.

Sincerely,
Thurgood Marshall

Stanley Belden to Thurgood Marshall
May 29, 1941
Dear Friend Marshall:
I am here [Fresno, California] with my brother at present. Don't know just what I am going to do. I hope to practice

law here some day; but I have to put $100.00 to take the examination and have to take it just the same as if I had never practiced law; but the thing that I am afraid of is that the Secretary of the bar commission in Oklahoma, will not give me a proper letter of recommendation (he is a Legionnaire) and that is necessary for my admission to the bar here.

I will take care of the petition in error, and if you need thirty days extension of time to complete the brief I will get that for you. Now we have six months in which to file the brief from the 10th day of February 1941, and can get an extension of time.

Sincerely yours,
Stanley D. Belden

Thurgood Marshall to Stanley Belden
June 4, 1941
Dear Friend Belden:
I have just returned to the office for a short time and find your letter received May 29.

Although I hope to have the brief ready by the 10th of July, I think it wise that you secure an extension of time of at least 30 days in order that we may be protected. As it stands now, I have only been in the office for about 8 days in the past month or so and I am leaving immediately for Florida and Louisiana on other cases. Please let me know as soon as you get the extension of time.

I do hope that you will get a letter from the Secretary of the bar commission in Oklahoma which will enable you to practice in California. I am sure you are aware that all of us are genuinely interested in your welfare and are hoping for the best.

With best wishes, I remain,

Sincerely,
Thurgood Marshall
Special Counsel

Thurgood Marshall to Stanley Belden
July 29, 1941
Dear Friend Belden:

Thank you for your letter of July 26 which clears up everything. It has just been the question of my failure to understand the procedure in Oklahoma. Now that it is clear, I will begin work immediately on the brief and send you a copy of the first draft just as soon as it is completed. I would like very much to get it done before August 8th so that I can sneak away for a few weeks and hide.

With best wishes, I remain,

Sincerely,
Thurgood Marshall
Special Counsel

Roscoe Dunjee to Thurgood Marshall
August 4, 1941
Dear Thurgood;

Enclosed herewith is a copy of rules, Criminal Court of Appeals, Oklahoma. You will note that the same is to also be found in "44 Oklahoma Criminal Reports".

You are not going to have any trouble getting before this court. The presiding judge B. B. Barefoot, is a personal friend of mine. He told me just a few minutes ago to tell you that you would be given as much time as you wanted for oral argument.

I have known Judge Barefoot for the past fifteen years and he is a liberal of the first water. I sometimes go out to his office and talk an hour. The last time at his request. You can see you will have easy sledding so far as presentation is concerned.

You will have 60 days from the time you filed petition in error to prepare your brief and the state has thirty, according to the Judge.

Let me know what I need to do from time to time so I can keep the boys in high on this end.

Sincerely yours,
Roscoe Dunjee
Editor BLACK DISPATCH

W.D. Lyons to Thurgood Marshall
August 5, 1941
Dear Sir:
I received your letter and the money you sent to me. I assure you that I certainly do appreciate it. I am also indebted to you for the many other kind things you have done.

I am going to school each night and progressing nicely in all of the subjects that I am taking. In this way I feel that I can better prepare myself while confined in this institution. We have a very good school here, and as soon as I have reached the required grade level I am going to take one or two of the mechanical courses that are offered. Some of the courses that are offered are: Welding, Gas Engine, Type Writing, Agriculture, Book Keeping, Journalism, and Diesel Engine. Out of this assortment of subjects I hope to find one that I can use for a means of making a living in later years.

Thanking you again for the many kindnesses you have bestowed upon me, and wishing you continued success in your work. I remain,

Sincerely yours,
W.D. Lyons #42675

The white primary case in Texas had become a major embarrassment for the NAACP after their client revealed that he had tried to vote in the runoff election but not in the original primary. The court found that the plaintiff had no standing to bring the suit and dismissed his case. With his latest effort to win voting rights for black Americans thrown out of court, Marshall started over, finding a new plaintiff in Texas and suing in county court for his right to vote.

In addition to recovering from this setback, Marshall and the other attorneys on the Lyons case worked fast under a tight deadline to prepare an appeal. Marshall tried to locate court records that would prove that Bizzell had, strangely, never been tried for the heinous murder and was released on suspiciously low bail, but he was unsuccessful. He did succeed in getting the ACLU to join the case with a brief in support of Lyons. Needing more time to prepare his argument and manage the tedious logistics of preparing and copying the briefs and the case made and sending them—large, pages-long documents all—back and forth between Oklahoma and New York, he asked for an extension, which Judge Barefoot granted. In August, with the appeal filed, after untold hours working and traveling at an exhausting pace, Marshall went on a much-needed vacation.

By the late summer of 1941 the United States was heaving toward war. The Third Reich approached the zenith of its territorial expansion in Europe. With the Nazi threat felt acutely now even across the Atlantic, denunciations of fascism and "Hitlerism" had become de rigueur in mainstream American society. Ever attuned to trends in pop culture, NAACP executive secretary Walter White wrote to a friend, asking him for help preparing a pamphlet to call out American hypocrisy.

"It tells a story which, I know you will agree, would fit in very snugly with what is going on in Hitler's Germany today," White wrote. "Would you be willing to write in your inimitable fashion a forward to this pamphlet, calling on America to stop Hitlerism while we are opposing it abroad?" The pamphlet would tell the story of W.D. Lyons's ordeal in Oklahoma. The title, he said, would be "It Did Happen Here"—a reference to Sinclair Lewis's 1935 novel that imagined the rise of fascism in the United States and a liberal rebellion against it.

Secretary of Thurgood Marshall to W.D. Lyons
August 15, 1941
Dear Mr. Lyons:
Remembering your request that we send you a book, we are forwarding to you, under separate cover, the one titled "Up from Slavery" which is an autobiography of Booker T. Washington. We think you will like it.

Sincerely,
Secretary to Thurgood Marshall

Thurgood Marshall to Roscoe Dunjee
October 8, 1941
Dear Roscoe:
Thank you for your letter of October 3 concerning the Lyons case. You realize that none of us have any worry

about your being able to raise funds in Oklahoma for these cases and we have no worry about the funds in this case. We leave these matters to you, Williamston, Gilliam and the others.

As to the question of whether I am coming down to the trial, you may rest assured that I will be there unless the trains, buses, and planes all stop running and I break both legs. Soon as you get an idea of the date of the hearing please let me know so that I may plan my trip as far in advance as possible.

Sincerely,
Thurgood Marshall
Special Counsel

W.D. Lyons to Thurgood Marshall
October 29, 1941
Dear Mr. Marshall:

I received your letter of August 19th. I was very glad to hear from you and I appreciated the book very much. It was exceedingly interesting. I am getting along fine, holding my chin up, and trusting in you.

I talked with the sheriff of Hugo a few days ago. He said that if my case was reversed, the court at Hugo would not try me again; that I would be released.

Mr. Marshall, I realize that I am in debt to you already, for many kind things you have done for me, but there is one more thing which I wish to ask of you. It is for financial aid for me if and, when, I am released. Of course you realize that it would not be wise for me to return to Hugo. I should like to obtain transportation to Detroit, Michigan, where I believe I could easily obtain work, unless you could arrange for employment for me some other place.

I plan to get located some place first, and then send for my wife later, after I begin work. If you can arrange for such help after I get work. I shall hope to hear from you very soon.

I am yours truly,
W.D. Lyons

Thurgood Marshall to W.D. Lyons
November 3, 1941
Dear Mr. Lyons:
This is to acknowledge your letter of October 29.

We have filed the brief in your case, and have just received word from the Court of Criminal Appeals that the case will be argued during the January term of Court. Immediately after a decision in the case will take up the matters you mentioned in your letter.

Rest assured that we will do everything possible for you and your family.

Very truly yours,
Thurgood Marshall
Special Counsel

When the day finally came for a hearing on W.D. Lyons's appeal— it was ultimately extended to March 4, 1942—both of his attorneys appeared before the court to make oral arguments in the case. The small Court of Criminal Appeals courtroom was packed with onlookers, including "a mixed-race delegation of whites and Negroes from Fort Towson," according to a report in the *Chicago Defender,* a prominent African American newspaper whose editors determined that fact remarkable enough to report under the headline WHITES SEEK APPEAL FOR ACCUSED MAN. Vernon Colclasure, the brother of Marie Rogers and now president of the newly formed Fort Towson NAACP, was among those present.

In his remarks to the three-judge panel, Thurgood Marshall assailed Oklahoma justice. "The only evidence in this case is that on the day of the murder the defendant, W.D. Lyons, was hunting in the vicinity with a shotgun," he said. He fulminated against the lawmen who had tortured Lyons, and especially against one man in particular who, he said, had been dispatched to Choctaw County to take the heat off the convict camp where the real murderers lived, and by extension off the prison warden Jess Dunn and Governor Phillips himself: Vernon Cheatwood.

"I've been in many cases where confessions were involved, but this is the worst," he said. "Men like Cheatwood are a disgrace to the State of Oklahoma."

The warden—and by extension the governor and Cheatwood—"had an interest in the confession because his chain gang was on trial," Marshall said.

In his comments, assistant attorney general Sam Lattimore, representing the state, denounced that theory. "There's nothing in this record which would indicate the state was attempting to take the blame off the penitentiary," he said. "There's nothing in this record against a state convict camp."

For his part, Belden laid out the simple but essential component of Lyons's case, the crux around which his entire appeal would ultimately turn. The men who tortured Lyons when he first confessed were present for Lyons's second confession, he noted. Thus, Belden said, the "fear generated in the first confession carried over into the second," and if the first was inadmissible—which the court had determined it was—then the second ought to be as well.

———————

W.D. Lyons to Thurgood Marshall
March 16, 1942

Dear Mr. Marshal:

In writing this letter, I am requesting that you do me another favor. I am in debt sixty cents for newspapers and don't have any money to pay for them, so I will appreciate very much if you send me some more money. I shall be exceedingly glad if you cooperate with me in this matter.

I read an article in the newspaper last week and discovered that you and Mr. Belden did a good job in arguing my case. Trying to convince the judges that I am innocent. And if The National Association for the Advancement of Colored People is successful in securing my release, I will dedicate my life to a type of effort that will assist in fighting for the rights of Colored People.

What I plan to do if I am released, will be to finish up in a higher school. Of course we have a good school here, but our teachers aren't qualified to give the education that is required. Please tell me when you are expecting the ultimate decision in my case.

　　　　　　With every best wish, I remain: Yours very truly,

　　　　　　　　　　　　　　　　　　　　W.D. Lyons

Thurgood Marshall to W.D. Lyons
March 24, 1942

Dear Mr. Lyons:

This will acknowledge your letter of March 16.

As to your request for information relative to when Judge Barefoot will render a decision in your case, I regret that I cannot give you any information on that subject.

You know, of course, that the matter is being weighed by the Judge, and it is discretionary with him as to when he will issue an opinion. As soon as we receive any information in this connection, you will be duly notified.

We are enclosing our check for $5.00, which will, we hope, maintain your needs in the way of personal expenditures. You will appreciate, I am sure, that our budget is extremely limited and we are thus not in a position to make extensive contributions of this nature, much as we should like to be able to do so.

All good wishes for the successful outcome of your case.

Very truly yours,
Thurgood Marshall
Special Counsel

W.D. Lyons to Thurgood Marshall
September 12, 1942
Dear Mr. Marshall:

As I have not heard from you since last spring although I wrote you a letter several weeks ago, it is assumed that your delay in responding is due more or less to an oversight or some urgent business activities which have commanded your attention.

Nevertheless, my express purpose in writing you a letter is not only to let you know that I am well and am getting on fairly well, but to let you know that I am in need of a little money. Unfortunately, I am not making any money here, and it is for that reason that I turn to you for money enough to buy such incidentals as tooth-paste, soap and etc. in addition to newspapers from the colored press.

Of course, I realize that your funds for this purpose is very limited; and that small sums of money can be spared in such instance. Albeit whatever amount that you can spare me should be highly appreciated.

Will you let me hear from you?

With kindest regards and my best wishes to you, I am,

Yours very truly,

W.D. Lyons

Roscoe Dunjee to Thurgood Marshall
October 20, 1942
Dear Thurgood;

Stanley Belden has been drafted and is now in the army. What should I do in connection with local counsel? I will certainly need some one to file a motion in appeal, should the court rule against us.

Please give me some plan of action. The local attorneys have been a little hostile (Negro) since I hired Belden and had you come to the state.

Attorney M.L. Thompson, who was for several years the president of the branch at Wewoka is living here now. I am of the opinion I should use him.

Let me hear from you on this matter. Should I notify Judge Barefoot that Belden is gone and tell him to notify you when the decision will be rendered?

Sincerely yours,

Roscoe Dunjee

BLACK DISPATCH

Thurgood Marshall to Roscoe Dunjee
October 26, 1942
Dear Roscoe:

Thanks for your letter of October 20th, which I [received when I] finally returned to the office from Washington. I really do not know what to do about local counsel. What about Hall in Tulsa? At any rate I can say that you will have to be very careful who you pick and I most certainly will stand behind you in picking Hall because of his splendid record here in this office.

I think it will be wise for you to telephone Judge Barefoot and request him to notify me of the decision in the Lyons Case, which I hope will be made sometime before the war is over at least.

Sincerely yours,
Thurgood Marshall
Special Counsel N.A.A.C.P.

W.D. Lyons to Thurgood Marshall
December 21, 1942
My dear Mr. Marshall:

Although I dislike being a mendicant, it is a matter of sincere regret that I have to be a regular parasite upon you; but as I am in a position where I cannot secure funds for which to purchase necessary incidentals, I am asking you to forward to me a pen and pencil set and some money provided you have some to spare.

Of course I realize that I am abysmally in debt to you for the kind favors which have been given me. Too, I am aware of the fact that the N.A.A.C.P. funds are exceedingly limited, but as I have no immediate consanguinities who are in a position to succor me in this particular matter I am asking you to spare me whatever you can.

I wish to call your attention to the fact that I am writing this letter not only for you to accommodate me but to inform you as to how I am getting along as well. However, it is hoped that you are doing well; although I hope you are.

In your response to my inquiry, please inform me as to when you are expecting a decision on my case.

With kindest regards and my best wishes for your continued good health, happiness and prosperity throughout the new year, I shall ever remain.

Very truly yours,

W.D. Lyons

W.D. Lyons to Thurgood Marshall
March 3, 1943
My dear Sir:
No doubt when this letter will have arrived at your office, you will either be busily engaged in contemplation of the various legal documents and other business activities which command your attention, or else you may be at some distant city attending to matters of equal consequence. However the case may be, I seize this opportunity to write you an occasional letter not only to say "hello," and that I am getting on as well as could be expected in prison, but to inform you that my general funds which, as usual, consists of money that you usually send to me for the purpose of buying incidentals, is now depleted.

Insomuch as I realize that the Educational Funds used for this purpose has always been limited, I should be thankful to receive whatever sum of money that you can possibly bestow.

I should appreciate your thoughtful consideration of this matter.

With kindest regards and my best wishes to you for continued good health, success and prosperity as well as the advancement of the organization, I shall ever remain,*

Very sincerely yours,

W.D. Lyons #42675

---

* Marshall scribbled a note onto this piece of correspondence before filing it away: "We just sent him some money."

Thurgood Marshall to Roscoe Dunjee
March 8, 1943
Dear Roscoe:
What in the world is happening with the W.D. Lyons Case? It looks to me as though every case in Oklahoma has been decided but this one. I would appreciate it if you would telephone Judge Barefoot and ask him what is happening and let me know what he says.

Sincerely,
Thurgood Marshall
Special Counsel

Roscoe Dunjee to Thurgood Marshall
March 27, 1943
Dear Thurgood;
I called Judge Barefoot and talked with him about the Lyons case. The Judge said he had been delayed by the current legislature, now in session, but promised he would get on it and complete the decision as soon as possible.

I called his attention to the fact that the state conference meets the first week in May, and that I was anxious to have a decision prior to that time.

He promised me that he would render the opinion before the state conference, so that I at least have a rough date pegged.

Twice during the conversation Barefoot said; "I have done more work on this case than any I have ever tackled, and I want to discuss it with you after I have rendered the decision."

He was very cordial and my general impression is Barefoot is going to render a decision in our favor.

Sincerely yours,
Roscoe Dunjee
Editor BLACK DISPATCH

W.D. Lyons to Thurgood Marshall
April 12, 1943
My dear Mr. Marshall:
Not having received a response to my letter of the last ultimo, I am writing again and repeating the substance of my former letter. first, I wish to say that I am well and getting along just as may be expected for a person in prison, though I am still being a good boy and holding my chin up.

I am in a predicament. I am buying a radio on install-ment plan, which costs $13.00. I have paid $6.50, all the money I had. The remainder ($6.50) is to be paid monthly at the rate of $3.00, or I lose the radio. The next payment is due on the 27 of this month, and I have no way to obtain that amount. If sending me a little money doesn't hurt your purse, please forward to me whatever you can bestow. I should like very much to receive whatever you send me by the 5th of this month.

Do you expect a decision on my case very soon? If you do, let me know. Your response by return mail will be appreciated.

With all good wishes to you and the N.A.A.C.P., I am,

Very sincerely yours,

W.D. Lyons

Thurgood Marshall to W.D. Lyons
April 20, 1943
Dear W.D.:
The reason I didn't answer your other letter sooner was because of the fact that we have been quite busy on other matters. Please bear in mind that we have very limited funds in this office and we need practically all of our money for court cases.

I am, however, requesting that a check be sent to you for $6.50, the balance on your radio. I doubt we will be able to give you any more money for a little while.

We are expecting a decision on your case in the very near future.

Very sincerely yours,
Thurgood Marshall
Special Counsel

Judge Barefoot to Roscoe Dunjee
May 5, 1943
Dear Sir:
I am in receipt of your letter of April 28, and in reply beg to advise that the case of which you speak is now under advisement in this Court. It has been necessary for each of the Judges to examine the entire record in the case, because of its importance, and for this reason it is not likely that our opinion will be rendered within the time suggested in your letter.

Assuring you that this case is being given the attention which it deserves, and with kindest personal regards, I beg to remain

Very respectfully,
Bert. B. Barefoot
Judge Criminal Court of Appeals

P.S. Thanks for sending me the official program of the Ninth Annual Session of the Oklahoma Conference of Branches, N.A.A.C.P. I have noted the names of many of my friends upon the different committees, and I am sure that your meeting will be a fine success. B.B.B.

NAACP News Release

June 11, 1943

LYONS CONVICTION AFFIRMED BY COURT OF APPEALS

Choctaw County, Okla.—The conviction of W.D. Lyons for the crime of murder in Choctaw, County, Oklahoma, was affirmed this week by Judge B.B. Barefoot of Oklahoma Court of Criminal Appeals in one of the longest opinions on record.

Judge Barefoot in discussing the police tactics employed in obtaining the confession stated "We here unhesitatingly condemn the methods used." But in the next 42 pages the court justified the second confession made during the same day as admissible.

NAACP lawyers representing Lyons contended that at the time of the second confession Lyons was still suffering from the effects of the beatings and other intimidations inflicted on him prior to the first confession and pointed out, "The methods used to obtain the confession in the case have no parallel in American jurisprudence. Such treatment of an American citizen by officers of the State of Oklahoma strikes at the very foundation of the principles of democracy, now threatened from without as well as from within."

The NAACP attorneys filed this week a motion for rehearing as the motion is denied. Application will be made to the United States Supreme Court for a writ of certiorari.

Lyons was convicted January 31, 1940, of the murder of three white persons near Hugo, Oklahoma. The appeal raised the question of the conviction of Lyons on the basis of a confession extorted by force and violence. The brief for Lyons pointed out that the night before the confession was obtained Lyons was kept in a room in the court house during the entire night, and that during the period there was admittedly at least 12 officers and citizens in the room. One of the officers kicked the skin off the shins of Lyons' legs. Another officer kicked him in the stomach and blacked his eye. Other officers cuffed him about. All of the officers admitted that during the period they placed a pan of human bones in Lyons' lap and told him they were the bones of the people whom he was charged with killing.

W.D. Lyons to Roscoe Dunjee
June 12, 1943
Dear Mr. Dunjee:
Having read in a newspaper that the decision of my case was unfavorable, I am inclined to say that judge B.B. Barefoot made a great mistake in giving proper justice. He stated that a new trial would be of no benefit to me; that I would be sentence to die in the electric chair if I were retried.

My principle reason for writing you is that I wish to be informed as to whether my case will be appealed to the U.S. Supreme Court. The U.S. Supreme Court, I am sure, is the only court wherein Negroes may obtain justice.

I sincerely will appreciate the N.A.A.C.P.'s appealing my case to the U.S. Supreme Court.

With regards and my best wishes to you, the N.A.A.C.P. for a successful future, I am

Sincerely yours,
W.D. Lyons

Roscoe Dunjee to W.D. Lyons
June 14, 1943
My dear Mr. Lyons;
I have just read your letter and note all you say. I am delighted to know you desire that your case be appealed. I

have already given instruction to appeal the case and notice has been given to the court.

You may be assured that the Oklahoma Conference of Branches NAACP will carry your case direct to the Supreme Court of the United States. We have already won three cases identical in their nature to yours and I see no reason for the high court to reverse itself in your cause of action.

Attorney Belden, as I said a moment ago, has already given notice of appeal, and Thurgood Marshall, in our New York office is preparing the necessary legal papers. Judge Barefoot has granted additional time over the legal period to prepare the petition for a new hearing.

I want you to holdup under this trying ordeal realizing that the NAACP is going to do everything humanly and legally possible to secure the character of relief to which I believe you are entitled.

Sincerely yours,
Roscoe Dunjee
President

Roscoe Dunjee to Thurgood Marshall
June 14, 1943
Dear Thurgood;
I received the enclosed letter this morning from Thurgood Marshall.* You will recall that in the Jess Hollins case the defendant became alarmed and asked us to quit. We seem to have a different sort of client this time.

Will we need any additional authorization from Lyons? I want to be clear on this point. Is there a possibility of

---

* This is clearly a typographical error. He's referring to W.D. Lyons.

someone attempting to suggest he have the action dismissed? I think if you were to write him an encouraging letter saying you were going to bat for him in real style it might overcome any fright unfriendly influences might seek to instill.

Write me on this subject and any other point you believe I should be advised in developing this case.

Sincerely yours,

Roscoe Dunjee

P.S. You or I one should keep this letter in our files that Lyons has written.

NAACP Assistant Special Counsel Milton Konvitz to W.D. Lyons
June 16, 1943
Dear Mr. Lyons:

Your letter to Mr. Roscoe Dunjee, President of the Oklahoma Conference of Branches, NAACP, has been forwarded to us.

Our special counsel, Mr. Thurgood Marshall, is working on your case, and I want to assure you that the case will receive our best attention and efforts.

Mr. Marshall is at the present time out of town, and upon his return early next week he will communicate with you.

Yours very truly,

Milton Konvitz

Assistant Special Counsel

Roscoe Dunjee to Thurgood Marshall
June 22, 1943
Dear Thurgood;

I just returned from Stanley Belden's farm, where I took the petition for rehearing yesterday evening as soon as it arrived. Belden thinks the petition is adequate and covers the two main points raised in the appeal. He asked me to say he gave his okeah to same. I presume you will hear from Hall direct.

Belden, as you may know, was allowed to return home from the armed forces with the understanding he was going to farm. He is on a farm three miles out of the city.

Is there any costs that will have to be put up in connection with the rehearing? Let me know as soon as possible some of the things we will have to do here, in which there will be costs so that I may start the branches preparing for same.

Sincerely yours,
Roscoe Dunjee
Editor BLACK DISPATCH

Thurgood Marshall to Roscoe Dunjee
July 16, 1943
Dear Roscoe:

Your letter of June 22 has been called to my attention on my return to the office.

As to the Lyons case, I would appreciate it if you would check with Judge Barefoot as to the approximate time the motion for rehearing will be heard, pointing out to him that Lyons has been in jail for quite some time. We are anxious to have the case disposed of. We will of course take the case to the United States Supreme Court if our motion for rehearing is denied.

As to the question of costs, there are no costs as of the present time. I will let you know whenever any additional costs come due.

Sincerely yours,
Thurgood Marshall
Special Counsel

More than three years had passed since the chilly Thursday evening in January when W.D. Lyons ducked out of his mother-in-law's house at dusk to take a nip of whiskey hidden in the woods and returned to be marched toward the ongoing nightmare he still lived every day. In those intervening 1,267 days, the world around him had been transformed.

Hitler, either directly or through alliances with client states and similarly fascistic regimes, controlled nearly the entire continent of Europe. Reliable reports had begun to percolate in the mainstream press suggesting that the full, gut-wrenching truth of the Nazi's ethnic cleansing campaign might be even worse than most imagined. Japan had bombed Pearl Harbor, drawing the United States finally and totally into the war, which brought unprecedented death and destruction to the islands of the Pacific.

Racial tensions roiled American cities as black soldiers fighting fascism abroad and black citizens supporting the war effort in factories at home refused to be treated as second-class citizens in their own country—in 1943 race riots erupted in Harlem, Los Angeles, Detroit, Mobile, and Beaumont, Texas.

In Oklahoma, however, 1943 seemed the start of a new and undeniably brighter era. The 1942 election—the first in which women were allowed to run for any office statewide—marked a sea change from the state's hard-tack frontier ethos to a more progressive and optimistic outlook. Governor Phillips had not sought reelection, and his successor, Robert S. Kerr (Oklahoma's first governor to have been born in the state), was a staunch New Deal Democrat who didn't share Phillips's combative style or his contempt for government aid and progressive policy. Rogers and Hammerstein's musical *Oklahoma!* opened in New York in March 1943 with explosive success and began its record-smashing run on Broadway. Oklahomans were so grateful for the production's cheerful, heart-warming portrayal of their state, in sharp contrast to the bleakness of Steinbeck's *Grapes of Wrath*, that, in later years, they took a number from the musical as their state song.

Change had come to the Oklahoma State Penitentiary too. Mere months after Lyons was convicted and transferred to the prison, a small group of inmates managed to take Warden Jess Dunn hostage and escape. Law enforcement pursued them, and Dunn was killed in the ensuing shootout. Dunn's legacy as warden lived on in the annual prison rodeo he'd started up in 1940—advertised as "the world's largest rodeo behind prison walls"—to which thousands from around the region came every year to see convicts ride broncos and bison, rope calves, and race horses. Like American society and culture on the outside, the war dominated life in the prison too. Some convicts volunteered to fight in exchange for early release, and a few did. A group of forty-four inmates serving life sentences volunteered to form a "suicide squad" that would go deep into Japanese-held territory to harass the enemy until facing almost certain death. The prison warden and the governor approved of the plan, and the crew even started training on the prison grounds, though in the end they did not deploy.

Lyons was not among those who volunteered, for he wasn't really a lifer. His case was still moving through the courts. He'd lost in the court of criminal appeals, but that was still in Oklahoma. He had a chance for a rehearing, and then he would appeal to the Supreme Court, where his famous, dashing attorney, about whom he read regularly in the newspapers, had won justice for many innocent black men just like him. His imminent release might come any day.

Whereas he had been kept in isolation at the start of his incarceration, he was now integrated into the prison's general black population. Lyons lived with perhaps three other convicts in a cell with a commode, a sink, a bunk, and a writing desk of his own. He was allowed three sets of clothes and two cubic feet of personal property, such as soap, tobacco for cigarettes, and his new radio, plus up to one cubic foot of reading material. He rose in the morning with the rest of the prison at around dawn, ate breakfast in the dining hall with the other black prisoners, went out to a work assignment until 3:30, and then he and the rest returned to the main prison for dinner and free time in the evening before lights out at 9:00 PM.

He'd been incarcerated a long time now, more than three years, but W.D. Lyons hadn't been wasting his time. When he went to jail he was nearly still a teenager, a poor young black man in a Jim Crow world. He'd already done a stint in prison, hadn't finished high school, and neither knew nor thought much about the world beyond the fifteen-mile stretch of rural Oklahoma that separated Hugo from Fort Towson. But in the prison at McAlester he'd been studying hard, eagerly preparing for the day he was finally released. The development of his mind over the years is evident in his penmanship and in the grammar, syntax, and content of his correspondence: over the years he matured from the sparse, child-like literacy of his lonely early letters, to the adolescent excitement of an expanding mind, on display in overwrought prose sprinkled with the biggest, fanciest dictionary words he could muster, to cleaner sentences and more high-minded, adult concerns, like getting money for newspapers and a radio, and finally, a few days shy of the Fourth of July, 1943, to this:

W.D. Lyons to Thurgood Marshall
July 1, 1943
Dear Mr. Marshall:
Amid the fierce struggle of human existence, and the uncertain life of today, I sense a growing wave of unrest

and dissatisfaction among colored people as a result of the undemocratic practices persistently employed by the dominant race to terrify, harass, disenfranchise, depress, segregate, and discriminate economically, educationally, and socially against the largest minority group of people in America. These undemocratic practices are not only inconsistent with the Declaration of Independence, but are a farce, and falls far short of the Declaration of the Rights of Man, and such democratic policies effecting the rights and liberties of a free people incorporated in a post war world.

It is the unscrupulous employment of such inequities to the extreme that great consternation of a revolutionary aspect sweeps the nation, pointing conclusively to the fact that bull[y]ing and brutality have taken the place of decency, and barbarism and violence of the middle age[s] is threatening to destroy the civilization of the 20th century.

The dominant race is too quick to mistake our patience for weakness, and our silence and tolerance for acquiescence. But the wrong inflicted on our people is resented with towering indignation. Wronged hearts will not always accept scurvy affronts and injustices; men will not always put up with kicks when they want fair play.

The misfortune of the Negroes is in the color of their skin, and that alone. The Negro finds himself on an economical level so low that a life of comfort is almost impossible. No matter how noble his character or how perfect a gentleman he might be in his manners and conduct, because his origin is indelibly stamped upon his countenance, visible to all, a mark that always carries with it painful humiliation since it forever exposes him to the prejudices of white people. Everything he does is minutely examined; a trifling error in the toilet, which would be overlooked in a white expert shoemaker, would excite amusement in the case of a Negro apprentice and you would hear the remark: "What else do you expect?" In a few cases is he considered a man of the same capabilities as the white man.

It is common to see white communities that refuse to allow colored men to perform any but menial offices and then despise them as a race of menials incapable of equal opportunities. But this attitude tends to estrange Negro-white relationship and makes harmony and co-operation impossible.

The solution to this problem is not social equality and marriage. Rather it is one of granting those basic human rights without which human life is impossible. Those basic human rights are as follows:

1. Equality of rights to live notwithstanding the various unequal qualities of individuals who should all be deemed absolutely equal before the eyes of the law.
2. Equality of freedom and protection against mob violence, torture, and any other form of ill-treatment.
3. Equality of rights to purchase property, and to enjoy personally property lawfully possessed.
4. Equality of rights to move freely about the community, nation, and world at his own expense.
5. Equality of rights to work in any lawful occupation or employment which he feels himself capable to perform.
6. Equality of rights to the utmost freedom of expression.
7. Equality of rights to better housing, sanitation, and health.
8. Equality of rights at the polls and in law-making.

These are the inalienable rights of every human being.
These, our common rights, which as the poet said, "Shines
ever there above, unextinguished and inextinguishable, like
the eternal stars above."

Very respectfully yours,

W.D. Lyons #42675

When W.D. Lyons wrote that unprompted letter to Thurgood
Marshall, there was no civil rights movement as such in the United
States. Emmett Till was barely a toddler, and it would be more than
a decade before his brutal murder in Mississippi helped galvanize
black Americans and their allies into a mass, peaceful insurrection
against white supremacy. Martin Luther King Jr. was still a preco-
cious high school student in Atlanta. Malcolm Little was a teenager
and a petty criminal in Harlem—he hadn't yet gone to prison,
joined the Nation of Islam, and adopted the name Malcolm X.

It's an extraordinary document, and not only because of the
way in which Lyons—who entered prison barely able to write a
letter asking for tobacco money—has grown as a writer into his
terse, muscular voice, with clear sentences of varied structures, all
methodically layered into a powerful treatise. He cites the Declaration of Independence but also the Declaration of the Rights of
Man, a seminal document of the Enlightenment produced in 1789
by the French National Constituent Assembly at the outset of the
French Revolution. His closing line makes reference to Friedrich
Schiller's 1804 play *William Tell*, about the Swiss folk hero's fight in
the late Middle Ages against Hapsburg tyranny. But that's not all.

From the translation he quotes it's clear Lyons isn't just citing
Schiller—he's quoting a line in which Schiller is quoted in the
English translation of a novel by Jose Rizal, the national hero of

the Philippines, called *El Filibusterismo*, the sequel to *Noli Me Tángere*. Together the two books formed the literary foundations of the Philippines' anticolonial insurrection in the nineteenth and twentieth centuries against Spanish and then American imperialism. What's more, he slightly misquotes the line—"inalienable rights, which, as the German poet says, shine ever there above, unextinguished and inextinguishable, like the eternal stars themselves," in Rizal's text. When Lyons sat down at a typewriter to express his thoughts about black liberation in a letter to Thurgood Marshall, and reproduced, in his own diction, a line from a work of anticolonial, revolutionary nineteenth-century Filipino literature, he did it from memory.

His sense of a growing wave of unrest among black Americans portends the civil rights movement, but Lyons goes further still. His solution "is not social equality and marriage." It's something far more elemental: not a request, but a demand; not for compassion, but dignity; not for equality, but rights—the inalienable rights that belong to every human on account of their humanity. He dissects the intricate maze that is life with black skin under a regime of white supremacy with uncanny sophistication for a man who very likely had never read a book just a few years earlier. His exploration of these themes places him in a lineage of African Americana extending from Frederick Douglass to W. E. B. Du Bois, right up to Richard Wright. Lyons had faced the awful weight of white supremacy at its most barbaric and lived to tell the tale, and he was more X than King. By 1943, with his case in limbo as he requested a rehearing at the appellate court before making his final stand at the Supreme Court, W.D. Lyons was ready to get out of prison and join—perhaps even help lead—the fight for black liberation.

NAACP Assistant Special Counsel Milton R. Konvitz to
W.D. Lyons
July 14, 1943
Dear Mr. Lyons:
Supplementing our letter to you of July 8, we wish to say
that we found your letter of great interest. We hope that
eventually you will win your freedom and will be able to
join our struggle for the rights enumerated in your letter.

   With all good wishes, I am

                                        Sincerely yours,
                                        Milton R. Konvitz
                                        Asst. Special Counsel

Roscoe Dunjee to Thurgood Marshall
July 22, 1943
Dear Thurgood;
Enclosed is a copy of the court minutes in which the
rehearing in the W.D. Lyons case was denied.

   Barefoot called me yesterday and again said he wanted
to talk with me about the case, but I have not business
myself to go out for the reason I assume [he] wants to
dissuade me from further defense. I can see nothing else.

   If you want additional time in preparing the writ Barefoot indicated you might have it. He in fact said so, so that
if you are pushed and need extra time ask for it.

   The minutes were addressed to Belden but he asked me
over the telephone this morning to send them direct to you.

                                        Sincerely yours,
                                        Roscoe Dunjee
                                        President
OKLAHOMA CONFERENCE OF BRANCHES NAACP

W.D. Lyons to Thurgood Marshall
July 31, 1943
My dear Mr. Marshall,
Notwithstanding the fact that the criminal court of appeals denied the petition for a rehearing of my case, the N.A.A.C.P., it was stated, will immediately file a writ of certiorari in the Supreme Court of the United States in Washington, D.C. Although the criminal court of appeals sustained the conviction of the lower court, it cannot prevent justice from being done, for the N.A.A.C.P. never quits a case.

My reason for writing this letter is that I demand to know about how long it will take the case to go through the U.S. Supreme Court. Give me your estimation.

Hoping your success, happiness, and prosperity, I am
Yours very sincerely,
W.D. Lyons #42675
P.S. Tell Mr. Konvitz that my reason for not replying to his letter of July 14 has been due to the fact that the postmaster has not given me permission. I will communicate with him as soon as I am given the opportunity.

Milton R. Konvitz to Thurgood Marshall
August 6, 1943
Dear Thurgood:
We have a letter from W.D. Lyons, saying that the Criminal Court of Appeals has denied the petition for rehearing, and he wants us to file a petition for a writ of certiorari to the Supreme Court of the United States.

Do you want me to write to Barefoot, asking him if the court has decided the matter?

Hope you have not overeaten of your mother-in-law's cooking. I am especially afraid of that dish of shrimps cooked in beer. Boy, am I glad I'm both allergic and kosher.

Sincerely yours,
Milton R. Konvitz

W.D. Lyons to Thurgood Marshall
August 17, 1943
Dear Sir:
Thank you for the money order in the amount of $6.50 which reached me August 16.

You may rest assured that I appreciate everything that is being done for me by the N.A.A.C.P.

Hoping you a successful future, I am

Yours very truly,
W.D. Lyons #42675

Roscoe Dunjee to Thurgood Marshall
August 19, 1943
Dear Thurgood;
Here's a stump buster. We have a divided court. Judge Thomas H. Doyle filed this dissent to the Barefoot opinion in the Criminal Court of Appeals Wednesday and the clerk of the supreme court sent this copy of the opinion to Belden in care of me this morning.

I have already shown the opinion to Belden and am sure you will be delighted to know that Doyle has decided with you on the main points raised in the rehearing petition.

I have ordered the clerk to proceed with the certification of the record as indicated in recent telegram.

Sincerely yours,
Roscoe Dunjee
Editor BLACK DISPATCH

12

For W.D. Lyons's attorneys and supporters, the 2–1 decision
reached by the Oklahoma Court of Criminal Appeals in his
case was as infuriating as it was perplexing. The essence of Judge
Barefoot's ruling, released in June 1943, held that when, during the
trial in Hugo, Judge Childers ordered the jurors out of the courtroom and heard testimony about W.D. Lyons's treatment at the
hands of the authorities, he sufficiently considered the question of
whether or not Lyons's second confession was admissible as evidence. Rather than issue a ruling on whether or not the confession
was admissible, Judge Barefoot ruled simply that the lower court
had done its job and followed the law, and that whatever decision Childers came to was thus appropriate. But rather than stop
there, the judge Dunjee had proclaimed a "liberal of the first order"
issued a defense of Choctaw County justice that approached the
line of absurdity and barreled right past it.

"The defendant was not rushed into a trial without adequate
preparation, but was given a delay of over one year," Barefoot wrote,
contending that the months on end that Lyons languished in jail without being brought to trial were for his own benefit. "The trial court
gave the defendant every consideration and right to which he was
entitled. The record presents as fair a trial as we have ever observed."

But if Barefoot's decision caused them dismay, Lyons's legal
team still saw a bright ray of hope in the dissenting opinion issued

by Judge Doyle. In strong, unambiguous language, Doyle found that Lyons had not received a fair trial and that his second confession—the one upon which his conviction depended—was obtained improperly and could not be used in evidence. "The well established rule is that if a confession has once been obtained through illegal influence, it must be clearly shown that such influence has been removed before a subsequent confession can be received in evidence," Doyle wrote. In other words, once the beating began, any confession the authorities got out of Lyons thereafter should be assumed to have been coerced and thus inadmissible, unless the state can prove otherwise. Here, for the first time in an official legal opinion in the *Lyons* case, a judge was articulating Marshall's point for him.

While Lyons watched his time behind bars turn into years, Marshall wasted no time in preparing an appeal to the Supreme Court of the United States. But the days dragged on nonetheless. With a huge case file needed to present to the Supreme Court, Lyons's attorneys corresponded feverishly to decide what precisely they needed to include—the cost of creating copies of a document so large was no small matter. Marshall prodded Oklahoma's assistant attorney general Sam Lattimore to come to an agreement on what facts they could agree on in order to shrink the size of the case file still more. All the while, Lyons's supporters and attorneys strategized about how to approach their day in front of the Supreme Court. Correspondence on these and other matters created yet more delays before the court finally agreed to consider Lyons's appeal—they set a hearing for early the following year.

While 1943 crawled toward 1944 the world at war continued to change with unusual intensity. The tide in the war turned decisively as the Allied fight against fascism gained steam. In Europe, the British Royal Air Force began bombing Berlin, the very heart of the Third Reich, while Mussolini's regime collapsed and Italy surrendered. Momentum was with the forces of liberal democracy, but there was still a long and arduous road ahead. On the home front in the United States, rationing of food and other goods escalated. Thousands of young men were still coming home from the war every month disfigured and damaged, or dead. Racial tensions ran high. On August 1, in the stale heat of the New York City summer, a white police officer shot a black soldier, setting off a deadly race riot in the streets of Harlem.

Though he was nearing the end of his fourth year behind bars, W.D. Lyons's spirits remained defiantly high. His legal team was among the finest in the country, and at the Supreme Court of the United States—arguing fundamental questions of constitutional rights and principles—they truly shone. His champion had lost plenty of cases in lower courts around the country tainted by the Jim Crow social order and corrupt local politics only to prevail in the nation's highest court. In that hallowed institution, where the purity of reasoned legal argument remained sacrosanct and uncorrupted—as in the lines from Rizal's translation of William Tell, "unextinguished and inextinguishable, like the eternal stars above"—Marshall had never lost.

For Marshall, however, this was novel territory. He'd been involved in numerous cases before the Supreme Court but nearly always under the guidance of his mentor, Charles Houston. The previous year Marshall had argued and won *Adams v. United States*, overturning the rape convictions of three black soldiers stationed in Louisiana. In January 1944, he was set to argue only his second case without Houston before the country's high court, *Smith v. Allwright*—the Texas white primary case he had been working so long to bring before the United States' arbiters of the law.

W.D. Lyons to Thurgood Marshall
December 14, 1943
Dear Sir:

It is with great pleasure that I seize this opportunity to wish you the very merriest Christmas. Moreover, I hope the New Year will be to you as successful as or more successful than the years bygone.

Hoping your success, happiness, and prosperity, I am

Very sincerely yours,

W.D. Lyons

P.S. To the N.A.A.C.P. can I wish nothing better than that it grow, prosper, and progress and that good health, happiness, and prosperity of each member be proportionate to the efforts of all.

W.D. Lyons to Roscoe Dunjee
February 10, 1944
Dear Mr. Dunjee:

Will you please inform me as to when you think the U.S. Supreme Court will hear my case. I read in the Black Dispatch last January 1 that my case would be argued this month, but have heard nothing else.

Give me your estimation of the time you think it will take the U.S. Supreme Court to render its decision after the case has been argued.

You may rest assured that I sincerely appreciate everything the N.A.A.C.P. is doing for me.

Very sincerely yours,

W.D. Lyons

Lyons would have to wait a while longer for any substantive update. While the Supreme Court continued inching back the scheduled date for his hearing, the attorneys on both sides of the case continued working to shrink the case file by coming to agreement on a set of undisputed facts. Marshall got curious about what happened to "Vernon Cheapwood [*sic*]? We want to know where he is and exactly what he is doing."

Dunjee wrote back, correcting Marshall to remember the man's name was "Cheatwood" and notifying him that after some good old-fashioned shoe-leather reporting, Dunjee had finally decided to just call up his wife at home and ask. Cheatwood, he reported, had served out the Phillips administration, but his employment with the state government was terminated after Kerr came into office. He got a job with the Pullman Company.

After months upon months of delay, the Supreme Court clerk finally contacted Marshall directly with a one-sentence letter: "Counsel should be present on Tuesday, April 25th, for the argument of the case of Lyons v. State of Oklahoma, No. 433, October Term, 1943 [*sic*]."

The air in Washington, DC, was thick and wet as Thurgood Marshall arrived confidently at the Supreme Court building across the street from Congress on Capitol Hill, on April 26, 1944. Rain dappled the building's wide marble front steps, but the pediment kept its rows of hulking columns dry and its enormous bronze front door draped in shadow.

Mere weeks earlier Marshall had won a major victory at the Supreme Court in *Smith v. Allwright*, and the NAACP still hummed with confidence following that hard-fought triumph, which ended the white primary system in Texas and beyond.

Lower court opinions on Lyons's case aside, Marshall knew that with the precedent he helped create through his win in *Chambers* he had case law on his side. The case he'd taken on nearly four years earlier, a case he'd always thought might end at the Supreme Court, had finally arrived there. He was thirty-six, in his element with the wind at his back, and in full command of his swagger. The day was his.

In his oral argument, Marshall stuck mostly to the fundamentals of the argument he'd been making all along: W.D. Lyons's conviction was based almost entirely on a confession that had been obtained through the use of torture and was therefore inadmissible. Without that confession, Marshall contended, there was no case against Lyons, and his client ought to be set free.

Though he had wanted to, Marshall was not able to argue a wider ranging defense, raising questions such as what became of Van Bizzell, who had been arrested for the same crime as Lyons but set free without ever being brought to trial, or the white convicts from the prison camp, whose confessions had been reported on in detail in the local newspaper. The question before the Supreme Court was not determining if W.D. Lyons was guilty or innocent but determining whether or not Lyons had received a fair trial in accordance with the US Constitution. If he had not, then the high court might overturn the lower court's decision. If he had, then the lower court ruling would stand.

These strictures didn't prevent the exchange during oral argument from straying a bit from the essential question at hand. While Marshall stood before the nine black-robed justices and responded to their queries about the case, Justice Owen Roberts, who lived part-time on a farm near Valley Forge, Pennsylvania, probed Marshall about Lyons's claim that he'd had a shotgun with him because he'd been rabbit hunting on the day of the murders.

"What size shot was he using?" Roberts asked.

"I understand it was number four," Marshall said.

"Number four is pretty big shot for rabbit hunting, isn't it?"

This set off a hushed commotion among the justices. Justice Stanley Reed leaned over to murmur a few questions to Roberts. "Chief Justice Harlan Stone, an expert fisherman," reported a tongue-in-cheek newspaper column about the exchange, "joined in the whispers."

Roberts nodded his head up and down soberly, knowingly.

"He seemed to know what he was talking about," the columnist wrote, "or at least there were not enough rabbit experts on the bench to dispute him."

"However," the column continued, "rabbit experts on Capitol Hill say that Justice Roberts probably was looking at the matter from the perspective of a gentleman farmer, not of those who shoot rabbits to eat. In this segment of society, they say, it isn't unusual to hunt rabbits with No. 4 shotgun cartridges."

W.D. Lyons to Thurgood Marshall
May 25, 1944
Dear Mr. Marshall:
As I desire information concerning my case, I am requesting you to inform me as to when you think the decision of the U.S. Supreme Court will be handed down.

I read in the daily papers that the case was argued last April 24 [*sic*], but have heard nothing more.

Your prompt consideration of this matter will be appreciated. Respectfully yours,

W.D. Lyons

Thurgood Marshall to W.D. Lyons
May 29, 1944
Dear Mr. Lyons:
Your case was argued, and we are hoping for the decision
some time within the next two weeks.

Very truly yours,
Thurgood Marshall
Special Counsel

13

IN EARLY JUNE 1944, the country's attention was fixed intently on events in Europe, where the Allies were advancing fast on disintegrating fascist forces. On June 4, the Allies marched virtually without resistance into Rome. At the opposite corner of Europe, nearly 160,000 Allied troops had assembled in England, preparing to cross the English Channel to the beaches of Normandy the following day. When the radio waves weren't filled by reports of Allied victories in Europe, they carried tunes in Bing Crosby's rich, earnest baritone, and Ella Fitzgerald's crisp, jazzy tremolo.

The papers on June 5 didn't carry news of the Allied invasion. Owing to a forecast for bad weather over northwestern France, the Allies postponed the planned invasion for twenty-four hours. But for Thurgood Marshall and the others at the NAACP—and for their twenty-five-year-old client serving a life sentence for murder at the Oklahoma State Penitentiary—June 5 brought dispiriting news.

NAACP executive secretary Walter White, who was in Washington, DC, when the court issued its verdict in the *Lyons* case, sent a telegraph by Western Union immediately to the national office as soon as he received word of their decision.

Walter White to Thurgood Marshall
June 5, 1944
WESTERN UNION TELEGRAM
LYONS CONVICTION AFFIRMED SIX TO THREE RUTLEDGE
DISSENTED. VIGOROUS DISSENTING OPINION BY MURPHY
AND BLACK.

WALTER WHITE

In the years since *Lyons v. Oklahoma*, legal scholars have struggled to understand how the court reached the decision it did.

One view blames Thurgood Marshall for doing a poor job in presenting the case, chiefly because in the brief he filed with the court he did not make a distinction between "disputed facts" and "undisputed facts." In cases like *Lyons*, it was common practice at the Supreme Court to distinguish between which facts were in dispute and which weren't—Marshall knew this and had made that exact distinction when preparing briefs for the Supreme Court before, though he did not do so in the *Lyons* case. But there's a simple explanation that legal scholars have missed: Marshall may have made no such distinction because all the facts in the record he presented to the court were undisputed. In order to save time and money by cutting down on the size of the case made to file with the Supreme Court, he had spent weeks going back and forth with attorneys for the state of Oklahoma to agree on a set of facts neither side denied. The court's majority opinion doesn't cite his failure to make this distinction, and the justices would presumably have been aware that the facts of the case they were working with had been presented to them in undisputed form.

The court's majority opinion was written by Justice Stanley Reed, a Kentucky native who rose to the lofty position of US solicitor general and then Supreme Court justice despite having attended but not completed law school. Reed addressed the issue narrowly. The question before the high court, he argued, was simply whether or not the trial court had sufficiently considered the admissibility of Lyons's second confession. It was not, he contended, the Supreme Court's place to apply the Fourteenth Amendment's equal protections clause to weigh whether or not Choctaw County law enforcement had violated W.D. Lyons's right under the Fifth Amendment not to be forced to incriminate himself. If the state court followed its own rules in assessing if a confession was legal or not, that was enough.

The crux of his argument came down to a question in American jurisprudence as old as America itself: Where does the authority of the federal government end and that of the states begin? For the Supreme Court, the question had come to be framed primarily in terms of the "incorporation debate"—did the Fourteenth Amendment's sweeping language incorporate the protections described in the Bill of Rights for the states too?

> All persons born or naturalized in the United States, and subject to the jurisdiction thereof, are citizens of the United States and of the State wherein they reside. No State shall make or enforce any law which shall abridge the privileges or immunities of citizens of the United States; nor shall any State deprive any person of life, liberty, or property, without due process of law; nor deny to any person within its jurisdiction the equal protection of the laws.

The Bill of Rights is less a list of rights than a list of limitations on what the government can do: "Congress shall make no law respecting an establishment of religion," etc. For the United States' first half century in existence those limitations were generally presumed to apply to the federal government but not the states themselves. After the clash of interests between the federal government and the states reached its zenith in the Civil War, Congress passed two amendments to the Constitution in short order: the Thirteenth Amendment, to abolish slavery, the principal issue over which the war had been fought, and the Fourteenth Amendment, to ensure that freed slaves and others living in the former Confederacy (and throughout the United States) would enjoy the protections guaranteed to American citizens by the Bill of Rights.

With the end of Reconstruction, when the federal government pulled troops out of occupied states that had taken part in the rebellion and communities throughout the South reimposed white supremacy, Fourteenth Amendment protections were scaled back dramatically. In the decades thereafter, the Supreme Court was occasionally presented with the question of whether or not the Fourteenth Amendment meant the limitations of governmental power applied to states' government as well, typically deciding, in deference to the political and cultural power of southern states, that it did not.

Beginning in the early 1940s, the incorporation debate heated up again in an increasingly divided court split between an anti-incorporationist bloc, led by Austrian-born Justice Felix Frankfurter, and an incorporationist bloc, led by Justice Hugo Black, a titan of American civil rights jurisprudence and one of the most influential justices in American history. From 1940 to 1943, divided decisions coming out of the Supreme Court (those involving a dissenting opinion rather than unanimity) jumped from 28 percent to 58 percent, the first time in the court's history that a majority of its decisions were divided. In this early iteration of the incorporation debate, the court decided the Fourteenth Amendment did not extend the constitutional right to due process to W.D. Lyons in his interrogations by Oklahoma officials, siding squarely on the side of what in the coming decades would generally be described as "states' rights."

The court's decision against Lyons may have come as such a shock to Marshall because mere months before the *Lyons* decision came down, the court issued a ruling with nearly opposite logic. In *Ashcraft v. Tennessee*, the court found that by aggressively interrogating a man, E. E. Ashcraft, for thirty-six hours with no sleep (he did not claim the authorities physically beat him), the police had extracted a coerced confession from him. The court also ruled in that case that the Fourteenth Amendment did incorporate the Fifth Amendment's prohibition on coerced confessions, and that it had the authority to reverse the state court's decision, which it did. It's difficult not to see entrenched racism at work when one reflects that the only key differences between *Lyons* and *Ashcraft* were that what W.D. Lyons experienced was far worse and that E. E. Ashcraft was white.

In a roaring dissent authored by Justice Frank Murphy and joined by Justice Hugo Black, Murphy rejected outright the logic that led the court to approve the "flagrant abuse by a state of the rights of an American citizen accused of murder. . . .

"To conclude that the brutality inflicted at the time of the first confession suddenly lost all of its effect in the short space of twelve hours," Murphy wrote, "is to close one's eyes to the realities of human nature. An individual does not that easily forget the type of torture that accompanied petitioner's previous refusal to confess, nor does a person like petitioner so quickly recover from the gruesome effects of having had a pan of human bones placed on his knees in order to force incriminating testimony from him."

_____

Roscoe Dunjee to Thurgood Marshall
June 17, 1944
Dear Thurgood:

I want to talk to you about the Lyons case. I am terribly depressed at the decision and yet there is a little spark of hope emanating from Hugo.

[Vernon] Colclasure was up to the office yesterday and he advises the new county attorney of Choctaw County is with us and is willing to reopen the case provided we can present substantial new evidence. Colclasure seems to feel he has unearthed sufficient new evidence to satisfy the county attorney.

I am going to Dallas Friday morning and plan to return by way of Hugo and see how the county attorney talks. Colclasure will meet me there and I will have opportunity to see what his reaction is to such evidence as Colclasure may present. As soon as I have concluded this conference I will seek your advice as to whether the case warrants reopening. And I, of course, would want to go into detail with you respecting what Colclasure calls new evidence.

With every best wish I remain, Sincerely yours,
Roscoe Dunjee
BLACK DISPATCH

Thurgood Marshall to Roscoe Dunjee
June 21, 1944
Dear Roscoe:

We are preparing a petition for rehearing in the Lyons case and will send you a copy as soon as it is ready.

Please let me have the dope you uncovered in Hugo on your trip.

Sincerely yours,
Thurgood Marshall
Special Counsel

W.D. Lyons to Thurgood Marshall
June 29, 1944
Dear Mr. Marshall:

Although I have heard from you recently, I have not, until now, decided to write you a letter—not so much to be inquisitive, but rather to let you know that I am well and getting along tolerably fair.

However, I should say that the recent U.S. Supreme Court decision in my case was quite a shock to me. But I will not despair: neither will I give up hope because I still feel that truth and justice will win.

Of course, I have heard from Mr. Dunjee concerning the decision of that Court. Knowing the N.A.A.C.P. as I do and that it is not the characteristic of it to "give up" a fight for a righteous cause of justice, I must inquire, nevertheless, as to what steps or actions will be taken next in an attempt to bring about a favorable decision of the higher Court?

I should appreciate a letter from you at your earliest convenience in regards to this subject.

With kindest regards and my best wishes to you for continued good health and happiness,

I shall remain,
Very sincerely yours,
W.D. Lyons

The Supreme Court's ruling against Lyons had been wholly unexpected, and in its wake Lyons and his attorneys seethed against its finality.

Marshall would not—could not—accept that the court ruled as it did. Mere weeks after the decision came down he filed a petition for a rehearing. He invited the American Civil Liberties Union to file another brief in support, but the ACLU was less than enthusiastic about their prospects now that the court had reached its judgment. "Little more than lukewarm," is how ACLU secretary Lucille B. Milner described the opinion at the ACLU regarding their prospects in securing a rehearing. The attorney who drafted the ACLU's brief, she said, was "so certain from the court's decision that there is little or no likelihood of getting a rehearing [that] he thinks it is a wasted motion and it would add nothing to your petition." And yet Marshall pressed on, testament to how passionately and personally he and others at the NAACP had come to feel about securing Lyons's freedom—and perhaps testament to a measure of responsibility he carried for Lyons's incarceration after he and Belden chose not to explore overtures from the governor's office to secure their client's freedom.

Marshall did have some cause for hope. As more time passed since the Rogers murder and local officials were replaced by a new guard, more citizens of Choctaw County felt compelled to come forward on Lyons's behalf.

In mid-July 1944, Dunjee wrote to Marshall to say he'd had word that "at least half a dozen white witnesses have already gone before the county attorney in Choctaw County and have testified that to their certain knowledge W.D. Lyons did not commit the crime for which he was convicted and have named the person or persons who in their knowledge are guilty." Dunjee suggested statements from these citizens might be added to Marshall's request for a rehearing. And in any case, "the new county attorney is 100% with us," he said, adding that he "has tentatively agreed to call a grand jury." But Dunjee's excitement over the events transpiring in Choctaw County betray his underlying desperation. The odds that new evidence might be considered by the Supreme Court in a request for rehearing were near zero—the Supreme Court does not work like that.

––––––––

W.D. Lyons to Thurgood Marshall
August 30, 1944
Dear Mr. Marshall:
Perhaps my constant inquisitiveness is a nuisance to you. But as I have heard from none of my attorneys since the recent U.S. Supreme Court decision of my case, I am almost compelled to ask you for information respecting the next steps the National Association for the Advancement of Colored People is going to take in the fight for my freedom.

Several weeks ago I read in a newspaper that the N.A.A.C.P. and the American Civil Liberties Union would search for new evidence and reopen the case immediately, though I have heard nothing more. If that is a fact, I should like you to write me telling me what the attorneys contemplate doing next.

Wishing you success, happiness, and prosperity, I am

Very sincerely yours,

W.D. Lyons

––––––––

Marshall replied to Lyons, letting him know that a petition for rehearing had indeed been made in his case and was still pending.

On October 3, he sent Lyons five dollars for the prison commissary. Six days later the Supreme Court clerk's office sent a telegram to Marshall to notify him that the high court had denied Lyons's petition for a rehearing.

Within days of the Supreme Court issuing its decision, Lyons was visited by two mysterious special investigators from the governor's office (or two men masquerading as such). On October 12, he wrote to Marshall to tell him of the meeting. He'd been questioned about half an hour, he said. "They asked me some of the same questions that I was asked at my trial, and they also remarked that I might have to beat the electric chair again." The investigators, for unknown reasons, asked about Lyons's great uncle, as well as a white man Lyons didn't recognize.

"My visitors talked nicely," Lyons wrote. "They used no harsh words or made no threats. But before they left, they said that I would never be given clemency. I cannot tell you through the mail all that was said to me."

The full meaning of this meeting is unknown and unknowable today, but it would seem to suggest that even though a new reformist governor was in office, new law enforcement officials held power in Choctaw County, and prison warden Jess Dunn was dead, powerful political figures in Oklahoma remained invested in seeing to it that Lyons was held accountable for the Rogers murders.

Though evidence of local corruption, new favorable witnesses, and sympathetic local politicians could not turn the tide in Lyons's favor, he held out hope—even as Marshall became quiet, apparently resigned to the impossibility of reversing his client's fate.

W.D. Lyons to Thurgood Marshall
January 8, 1945
Dear Mr. Marshall:

As I wish to know more about the progress that is being made in my behalf, I should like you to inform me as to when you plan to reopen my case.

Mr. Ralph Jennings, who was elected county attorney of Hugo, the town in which I was convicted, visited me not long ago. He said that for the past six months he has been in search of a clue or clues that will guide him to the actual murderers responsible for the crime of which I'm serving a life sentence for, and that his effort to procure new evidence has resulted to the collection of nothing but rumors.

Your telling me something of the advancement that the N.A.A.C.P. is making in my behalf will be appreciated.

Very sincerely yours,
W.D. Lyons

W.D. Lyons to Thurgood Marshall
January 20, 1945
Dear Mr. Marshall:

Today I am mailing you a good looking hand-made pocketbook, which I intended to send you last Christmas for a present. I hope you will accept it as a Christmas present.

This pocketbook was made by one of the inmates of this prison. I hope you will like it. Wishing you success, happiness, and prosperity, I am

Very sincerely yours,
W.D. Lyons

P.S. I will send $50.00 to the national office of the N.A.A.C.P. within a few days or weeks. This money will be used in the fight for negro rights at home and abroad.*

W.D. Lyons to Thurgood Marshall
February 19, 1945
Dear Mr. Marshall:
Pardon me for intruding upon your valuable time, but I have decided to grasp this opportunity to write you a letter pursuant to my promise to write occasionally to inform you as to how I am getting on.

Happily, I am well and as usual, trying to make the most of life, and my condition. I have not lost courage nor hope. Therefore, it behooves me to say that I am doing as well as could be expected under the circumstances. May it be said of you that you are well and enjoying buoyant health and success.

Although I am hopeful and very much encouraged respecting the future, I feel inclined, nevertheless, to ask you certain questions with reference to future development of my case. I should welcome information relative to the "re-opening" of my case, a right which, I understand, the U.S. Supreme Court has already granted.

---

* During this period at the Oklahoma State Penitentiary, many prisoners began earning relatively large amounts of money selling handicrafts made in the prison craft center to people on the outside. The next prison warden to assume power soon cracked down on the practice, but for a short while convicts in McAlester had been able make a decent living from behind bars. Presumably this practice is the source of Lyons's fifty dollars.

Has any new evidence been uncovered, necessary for a new hearing of my case? If so, how long do you suppose it will be before my case shall be reopened and reviewed?

I should be beholden to you for your earnest and thoughtful consideration of this matter, and for your kindness I should be deeply grateful.

Very sincerely yours,

W.D. Lyons

Thurgood Marshall to W.D. Lyons
February 23, 1945

On my return to the office a few days ago, I found your very thoughtful present to me.

It is exactly what I have wanted for a long time but never seemed to get around to buying. The wallet is just the right size because I always have so many papers to carry around with me that I never have been able to find one that would hold them all. So you can see how much I appreciate your gift.

I hope this finds you well, and once again, my sincerest thanks. Sincerely,

Thurgood Marshall

Special Counsel

What Lyons is referring to in the letter above regarding the reopening of his case is unclear. The Supreme Court did not reopen his case or issue any official pronouncement indicating that it might. Perhaps he had spoken to Dunjee or another person invested in his case and misconstrued their attempts to see the matter revisited by the authorities in Choctaw County.

There is no evidence Marshall replied to any more of Lyons's letters until the short note thanking him for the pocketbook. Tellingly, in the pocketbook letter Marshall has nothing to say about Lyons's case, perhaps avoiding the subject because there was nothing to say, because there was nothing left to be done.

———————

W.D. Lyons to Thurgood Marshall
October 13, 1945
Dear Mr. Marshall:
I have recently read the interesting account and announcement of the 11th annual session of the Oklahoma Conference of Branches of the N.A.A.C.P. which is scheduled to convene at McAlester, Oklahoma, on November 1st and 2nd. I have also noted that such prominent figures as yourself, Dean Williams Pickens, Mr. Dunjee and many others will be present.

The great world conflict has ceased and it is hoped that this session will be more glorious and full of interest than the past session. Moreover, it is also hoped that you and others can and will find leisure time during recess to drive out here at the prison to see me. I should like very much to see you and Mr. Dunjee, and I take this means to give you a reminder —"Please do not forget me."

With kindest regards and my best wishes to you and yours for continued good health and prosperity, I am,

Very cordially yours,
W.D. Lyons

W.D. Lyons's mother, Rosie Fleeks, to Thurgood Marshall
May 24, 1946

Mr. Thurgood Marshall,

Dear Sir I am writing you about W.D. Lyons case I wants to know if there can be a way for him to get out of Prison he say he is tired of staying there and if it way he could get out he talk like he may hurt him self he say he is tired staying in Prison he wants to get out before the governor Kerr goes out of office I want to know from you What you do about the case Mr. Thurgood Marshall would there any way you could free him or parole him out of Prison if you can Write me at once and let me know please he wants to get out bad he say he is tired of Prison so I will close looking to here from you at once.

This letter is from W.D. Lyons mother. I wants my poor son out of prison. I know you can plan some way for him to get out. So write at once please I will close my letter answer soon from

Mrs. Rosie Fleeks

W.D. Lyons mother

I want to know if the NAACP could make a way to parole him out of prison soon. Write me please

---

An NAACP assistant attorney replied to Rosie Fleeks to let her know that though they had "worked very hard and diligently on your son's case" they had been unsuccessful. "There is nothing further that we can do," the attorney said. He suggested she write to the prison warden to ask when her son was eligible for parole and petition the Board of Pardon and Parole on his behalf. There is no evidence Marshall or other NAACP officers accepted Lyons's invitation to visit him during the upcoming NAACP conference to be held near the prison in McAlester. The fight to win Lyons's freedom by proving his innocence was effectively over.

Perhaps finally accepting his lot, Lyons appears to have stopped writing to Marshall or anyone else at the NAACP. He got a job in the prison laundry, where he ironed sheets, shirts, pants, and jackets for the rest of his stay at the Oklahoma State Penitentiary. He continued taking classes at the prison school, studying television repair in the 1950s.

In 1952, Lyons and another prisoner who became interested in his case wrote to the NAACP asking for Lyons's case file. Their efforts to reopen the matter went nowhere, but Marshall, inspired by Lyons's renewed interest in winning his freedom, wrote to Sam Lattimore, the deputy attorney general who had participated in Lyons's original trial, to ask if Lattimore had rethought his position that Lyons was "a pretty bad fellow." He asked if Lattimore might consider joining a petition for clemency. Lattimore wrote back curtly that such questions were for the Pardon and Parole Board, not him, but he didn't think they'd even consider it yet regardless. Neither Marshall nor anyone else at the NAACP replied, and thus ended the NAACP's involvement with W.D. Lyons.

Though not, by a long shot, with Oklahoma.

14

A T THE OKLAHOMA NAACP state conference held in McAlester, Oklahoma, in October 1945—a drive of less than five minutes from the prison where W.D. Lyons was confined—Marshall gave a rousing speech in which he laid out for the assembled delegates the NAACP's long-term strategy to undo separate but equal. If Oklahoma was going to have separate schools for blacks, then they had better be equal, he contended. But Oklahoma had no law school that allowed black students. Marshall urged the delegates to launch a direct assault on Oklahoma's segregated graduate schools.

If they could find the right plaintiff he was confident he could win this case, he said. "This is the easiest case to beat that ever entered the courts of Oklahoma," Marshall told the crowd, perhaps overstating his confidence a bit for this audience still smarting from his recent defeat in the *Lyons* case. "I could win this type of case even down in Mississippi." And thus began the search for a plaintiff to be the new tip of Marshall's spear in his long war to legally overthrow the separate but equal doctrine. This was not an easy task.

A spate of recent setbacks had shown just how taxing being the plaintiff in an NAACP lawsuit could be. Not only would that person need to have standing to bring a lawsuit—meaning, in this case, they would need to be qualified to attend graduate school and intent on finishing, and able to show they had been harmed by a state's separate and unequal graduate school offerings—they would also need to be prepared for a protracted legal battle, harsh public scrutiny, and perhaps even threats to their physical safety. The pressure could be intense, even in victory. After all, it was when Lloyd Gaines's quest for admission into Missouri's whites-only law school was going well that Gaines may have decided of his own accord to disappear without a trace.

The NAACP had "lawyers ready but [it did] not have the cases," Marshall wrote in a memo to Walter White at the time. He needed to find clients who were "in the fight as a matter of principle, and people who [would] undergo serious strains for matters of principle."

Dr. W. A. J. Bullock had an idea.

A doctor and pillar in the local black community in Chickasha, Oklahoma, Bullock was a highly active leader in the regional NAACP. He had advanced Stanley Belden that first $250 needed to print the transcript of Lyons's trial in order to quickly file his appeal. When Thurgood Marshall issued a memorandum in 1941 to branches across Oklahoma about the *Lyons* case and called for members to "BUILD A FUND FOR RACE DEFENSE!" donations were directed to Bullock's address.

Bullock was the family doctor of the Sipuel family, and after the McAlester meeting he visited their home in Chickasha to make a proposition. If their son, Lemuel—a star student, World War II veteran, and Langston University graduate—would attempt to enroll in the University of Oklahoma law school, the NAACP would vigorously represent him in court, Bullock promised. He cautioned Lemuel that the controversy would likely be long and bitter, and he raised the specter of Lloyd Gaines's disappearance to emphasize that the risks to self and sanity were very real. Norman, Oklahoma, where the university was located, was a college town second and a southern town first, of the sort where blacks were warned not to let the sun go down while they were still in the city limits.

After thinking it over a moment, Lemuel told Bullock that he wasn't the man for the task. He'd planned to attend Howard University's law school after graduating from college, and his army service had already delayed his education for three years. He was in a hurry to get on with it, he said. So he passed.

When Lemuel declined the offer, his younger sister's heart stirred. Recently married and just out of college, she was in a better position to handle the difficulties sure to come with suing the University of Oklahoma to force the law school to accept a qualified black student. She sat eagerly in electric silence for a few moments before one of her parents suggested she might be a good candidate. Bullock looked at her, asked if she was available for the mission, and she gave an enthusiastic yes on the spot. Bullock promised to bring this suggestion to Roscoe Dunjee and departed. When the door closed behind him, Ada Lois Sipuel Fisher danced in a circle and clapped her hands in celebration. She'd been preparing for this role her entire life.

The Sipuels had moved to Chickasha from Tulsa only a few years before Ada was born, after their home was destroyed in the days-long antiblack pogrom known commonly as the Tulsa Race Riot of 1921. Nearly a decade after the move, on May 31, 1930, Chickasha resident Henry Argo, a young black man, was accused of raping a local white woman and summarily sprung from jail and executed by a white mob. Ada's mother, Martha, helped lead the campaign to oust the county sheriff—To HELL WITH MATT SANKEY read her audacious homemade bumper sticker—and other political leaders who had been negligent, or complicit, in the Argo affair. Argo's was the last documented lynching in Oklahoma and a defining event in young Ada Sipuel's developing race consciousness.

There was also the fact that Ada Sipuel Fisher was already personally acquainted with the man who would be her attorney, though he did not know it at the time. She related the encounter in her autobiography: "I still vividly recall the time—I was in the seventh or eighth grade—when Dr. Bullock brought a NAACP representative to speak at Lincoln School. The speaker was in the state as part of his work, which included helping small chapters all over the country. In the main, though, he was a lawyer, only the second black lawyer I had ever seen. I remember seeing this one because he was the most handsome, articulate, brilliant, and charismatic man I had ever seen. Our speaker's name, Dr. Bullock told us in introducing him, was Thurgood Marshall."

Sipuel Fisher and her family closely followed Marshall's work in the trial of W.D. Lyons, and she later recalled how much his appearance in that Hugo courtroom had meant to young black Oklahomans at the time. Lyons's first defense fund had been established by John Worley, a white man whom Martha Sipuel helped elect mayor of Chickasha "after the Argo tragedy," she wrote. "The fund's first one hundred dollars came directly from the mayor's own pocket—perhaps payment in part for the debt owed Henry Argo's people." The ambition to find "a job like Thurgood Marshall's, that NAACP lawyer who had so moved me in junior high school," Sipuel Fisher wrote, had been her inspiration for attending law school in the first place.

On a cold January day in 1946, Ada Lois Sipuel Fisher traveled with Bullock and Dunjee to the University of Oklahoma campus where, as planned, she attempted to enroll in law school. She was denied acceptance, as she knew she would be, on account of her race. The trio drove back to Dunjee's office in Oklahoma City, where they called Thurgood Marshall to tell him the news. On the phone, Marshall explained to his new client that she would also be represented by Tulsa-based attorney Amos T. Hall, who would shortly be initiating the process of filing suit against the university's board of regents.

Her case went all the way to the Supreme Court, and this time Marshall won. After their protracted legal battle, in 1949, Sipuel Fisher enrolled at the University of Oklahoma law school. She graduated in 1951 and practiced law as an attorney for the NAACP in Oklahoma. In the early 1990s she accepted an appointment to the University of Oklahoma's board of regents—the very entity she had sued.

Sipuel Fisher's ultimately successful lawsuit to force the University of Oklahoma Law School to end its racist exclusion of black students was a major milestone in the NAACP's sabotage campaign to overthrow Jim Crow. In the *Gaines* case, the court had ruled that states had an obligation to meet the needs of black students, but the court's final ruling in *Sipuel v. Board of Regents of Univ. of Okla.* said Oklahoma had to meet her needs immediately. States had successfully used stalling as a tactic to maintain the Jim Crow social order for generations, and the decision in Sipuel Fisher's case, though it came after *Gaines*, was thus more consequential.

Sipuel established clearly that the constitution demanded either separate and truly equal schools or an end to segregation, and that the high court had lost patience with Jim Crow delay tactics. The case was also a much-needed morale booster, proving that being represented by the NAACP in a controversial case with major civil rights ramifications didn't have to end the way things ended for Lloyd Gaines or W.D. Lyons.

As law professor Cheryl B. Wattley wrote in an article about the Sipuel Fisher case for the *Oklahoma Law Review*, "She was the female David fighting the Goliath of an entrenched, deeply rooted social system. Though she may not have slain the giant of inequity and unfairness, she so pained the system of segregation that it would shortly succumb to the final blows."

Sipuel was decisive, but it did not create the sort of tectonic change that would be necessary to defeat Jim Crow. Similarly, the funds raised as a result of the *Lyons* case did not create a massive war chest out of which the group would fund its battles for decades to come. But each case was pivotal, coming at just the right moment to allow Marshall to keep the lights on and the momentum barreling forward.

In its own way, each of Marshall's Supreme Court cases propelled the NAACP toward *Brown v. Board of Education of Topeka*, in which, in 1954, the Supreme Court finally struck down the separate but equal doctrine altogether. In *Brown*, the court ruled that a segregated system was inherently unequal, that the Fourteenth Amendment demanded the equal protection of the laws for all citizens, and that segregated public schools were thus irredeemably unconstitutional. The fight to desegregate America's schools and public facilities—to say nothing of the minds and hearts of Americans—would drag on for decades more, and continues today, but *Brown* was D-day for the battle plan first conceived decades earlier by Nathan Margold and Charles Hamilton Houston to reshape the law from within and force the separate but equal doctrine to overthrow itself.

Houston did not live to see the final stages of his plan unfold. His death in 1950 was particularly difficult for Marshall, who would credit Houston in the decades to come as the real architect of the civil rights revolution the NAACP attorneys achieved.

Thurgood Marshall continued to litigate groundbreaking civil rights cases that reshaped American society—of the thirty-two cases he brought before the Supreme Court, he lost only three in all. He left the NAACP Legal Defense Fund in 1961 to accept an appointment from President John F. Kennedy to the Court of Appeals for the Second Circuit, where he served until President Lyndon Johnson made him the first African American solicitor general in 1965. In 1967, Johnson appointed Thurgood Marshall to the US Supreme Court. America's first black Supreme Court justice, Marshall spent more than two decades on the court as a fierce and consistent defender of civil liberties. He was a steadfast opponent of the death penalty, which, as he saw in his extensive travels across the country as a dogged young NAACP lawyer, was and still is disproportionally applied to black defendants.

Throughout his tenure on the bench, Marshall was an unwavering advocate for the rights of criminal defendants, not because of a penchant for leniency, but because real-life experience had shaped his understanding of the criminal justice system and its shortcomings. Unlike the vast majority of justices who have served on the Supreme Court, for Thurgood Marshall corruption and inequity in the criminal justice system were not academic abstractions. With his own eyes he had seen utter savagery masquerading as genteel civility. He'd seen the lives of innocent men and women broken under the wheel of business as usual, thoughtlessly discarded to preserve the status quo. He'd shaken W.D. Lyons's hand before watching a parade of upstanding Choctaw County lawmen lie on the witness stand to see him convicted. He'd corresponded with Lyons about his client's hopes and ambitions, about the struggle for black liberation, about the man Lyons might become once he was finally exonerated and set free. He'd read the plaintive, hand-scrawled letter from Lyons's mother begging, fruitlessly, for Marshall to conjure up a miracle to help her son.

Marshall understood the stakes at a visceral level that his colleagues on the Supreme Court did not, and he used his unique life experiences to enlighten his fellow justices. In a heartfelt essay about Marshall, Justice Sandra Day O'Connor recalled how he would regale the others with stories from his days in the trenches fighting for the persecuted and oppressed.

"His stories reflect a truly expansive personality, and the perspective of a man who immerses himself in human suffering and then translates that suffering in a way that others can bear and understand," O'Connor wrote. "Occasionally, at Conference meetings, I still catch myself looking expectantly for his raised brow and his twinkling eye, hoping to hear, just once more, another story that would, by and by, perhaps change the way I see the world."

Thurgood Marshall once promised an interviewer that he intended to serve out the entirety of his lifetime appointment and "die at 110, shot by a jealous husband." Sadly, he didn't make it quite that long. When Marshall retired from the Supreme Court in 1991 due to health problems, he was the highest-office-holding black American in history, a distinction eclipsed only by Barack Obama's election to the presidency in 2008.

Thurgood Marshall died in January 1993, at age eighty-four. He is buried in Arlington National Cemetery.

Underneath his contempt for the reactionary tendencies of the state's political class, Stanley Belden tended to a deep and abiding love for Oklahoma and its common people. After the Second World War he returned to the state from California to start an oil recycling cooperative—a bold proposition indeed in a state beholden to the oil industry.

But as America entered the Eisenhower years and settled into a protracted Cold War with the USSR, with his law practice ruined and his oil recycling venture unsuccessful, Stanley Belden finally gave up on Oklahoma. He and his wife, Gladys, moved to Eugene, Oregon, where they raised four daughters and a son. Belden's son, David, describes him as a loving but exacting father who demanded absolute excellence and moral rectitude from his children.

Belden became a chiropractor and a passionate organic gardener. He kept up his lifelong fight for social justice as an activist in the local civil rights movement, and in antiwar activism during the Vietnam War. As the years ticked by he let his beard grow long and white. In the 1980s, he became a dedicated antinuclear activist, and in 1988, on his ninetieth birthday, he was arrested while protesting a nuclear testing site in Nevada. He spent the night in jail.

In the summer of 1993, at the age of ninety-five, Stanley Belden's health began failing. A doctor gave him twenty-four hours to live, but he persisted for five more days while friends and loved ones came to pay respects. One of those visitors later recalled that on his deathbed, shortly before he passed, Belden looked up at him and asked, "Do you think I've done enough?"

Despite an unblemished record of behavior as a prisoner at the Oklahoma State Penitentiary, W.D. Lyons was not let out of prison when he first became eligible for parole in February 1956, after serving fifteen years of his life sentence. He lived behind bars for five more years, serving twenty years in total.

On the advice of the Pardon and Parole Board, Lyons was finally granted parole in 1961 by Oklahoma governor J. Howard Edmondson. Two days later, on May 20, 1961, on an overcast Saturday cooled and dampened by a steady spring rain, W.D. Lyons walked out of the thick white gates of the Oklahoma State Penitentiary for the last time.

Lyons moved to Okmulgee, a sizable town near Tulsa with a large black community. Before leaving prison he had arranged a job with the help of a local attorney, working as a farm laborer. He earned eighty dollars a month, plus a house to live in and groceries. In time, he got a new job earning $200 per month as a television repairman, using skills he had learned in the prison school. He remarried, and together he and his wife, Mildred, raised a son and a daughter.

In 1965, on the recommendation of the Pardon and Parole Board, Oklahoma's first Republican governor, Henry Bellmon, granted Lyons clemency with an official pardon. It is a coincidence, but a poetic one, that on the same day he granted Lyons clemency, the governor gave an order that officially ended the open range in Oklahoma, the policy whereby cattle could freely graze across open lands on the prairie. With the stroke of his pen, Bellmon declared the frontier in Oklahoma closed, and the wild soul of a once pastoral state was finally laid to rest.

On the day Lyons got out of prison, a mixed-race group of voting rights activists traveled at high speed down the highway on a bus toward Montgomery, Alabama. These Freedom Riders had encountered trouble over the preceding weeks as they traversed the South helping black citizens register to vote, but what awaited them in Montgomery was of a different order. As they reached the city limit, their highway patrol escort abandoned them. So did the police who were ostensibly deployed to keep the peace at the local bus station. When they came to a stop in Montgomery, hundreds of white citizens, including members of the Ku Klux Klan, besieged them with lead pipes and broken bottles, beating many of them into bloody heaps of broken bones and shattered teeth. The next day more mob violence roared through the city as white racists terrorized the activists. In Washington, DC, President John F. Kennedy, horrified by the violence and shamed by the outrage erupting across the country, inched closer to deploying federal troops to protect the Freedom Riders.

The mob violence in Montgomery was a pivotal episode at the outset of the American civil rights movement of the 1960s. Had Lyons won his appeal in the Supreme Court, one wonders if he—defendant in a famous criminal case, personally acquainted with the NAACP's superstar civil rights attorney Thurgood Marshall, reader of Jose Rizal, writer of stirring prose on race and liberation—might have been active in that movement. Perhaps he might even have been one of its leaders, an elder mentor to the younger Freedom Riders and their cohort.

But Lyons had emerged from prison a changed man. He made few friends in Okmulgee and socialized little. Many years later, his wife, Mildred, described an unkind, taciturn man who kept to himself even in his own home, except during weekly bouts of extreme drunkenness. After their kids were grown, Mildred left W.D., who moved into another house in Okmulgee a few blocks away.

In the early 1990s, W.D. Lyons suffered a stroke that left him paralyzed on his right side. On a damp and unseasonably hot spring day, April 15, 1994, Lyons was killed by a gunshot wound and his house burned down with him inside.

Mildred later said she believed Lyons, crippled by his recent stroke and thus probably unable to wield a gun himself, had been murdered by intruders. But in the official record of his death, the gunshot that killed him is reported as self-inflicted—his death, in other words, is recorded as a suicide. Either W.D. Lyons was shot and killed by an assailant who also burned his house down, or he set fire to his own home and killed himself in circumstances eerily reminiscent of the Rogers family murder for which he'd been wrongly convicted.

W.D. Lyons is buried in an unmarked grave in the shade of a tall and crooked old tree near the back of the African American cemetery in Okmulgee.

ACKNOWLEDGMENTS

THIS BOOK WAS first conceived by John Nicks—the father in this father-son writing team—nearly twenty years ago. As a project that has been so long in the making, it is especially difficult to fully account for the many individuals and institutions who made this book possible. We hope the fact that we have nonetheless tried will serve as testament to the immense gratitude we feel to the people—most of whom will, out of necessity, remain unnamed here—without whom this story would never have come to life.

The archives of the National Association for the Advancement of Colored People are a national treasure, and without the NAACP's generosity and foresight in making their archives public this book would, quite simply, not exist. We must also thank the archivists at the Library of Congress, the Oklahoma Historical Society, the Fort Towson Museum, the Choctaw County Library, and the sundry other research libraries around the United States whose records we consulted to answer questions large and small in the course of reporting this project.

We wish to say a special thank you to Mildred Lyons, whose insight into the central character of this story was invaluable. We are also grateful to the many residents of Hugo and Fort Towson who shared their memories of their towns and of the Lyons saga with us. On a similar note, we extend a special thanks to David Belden, the son of Stanley Belden, for generously telling us about his father. Thank you to Shirley and Wayne Wiegand for generously sharing their research about Stanley Belden; to Josh Jones for his assistance in organizing our research; to our agent, Jim Fitzgerald; to Yuval Taylor for his always wise guidance as our editor; to Bishop Thomas Smith, pastor for more than fifty years of the Church of the Living God in Tulsa, for his wisdom and perspective; to Percy Julian Jr. of Madison, Wisconsin, and Sherrilyn Ifill, current president of the NAACP Legal Defense Fund, for being inspirations to John as civil rights lawyers; to our wide circle of friends and family for their encouragement regarding this project over the years; and especially to Judge Linda Morrissey—John's wife, Denver's mom—to whom this book is dedicated, for her support, her patience, and for being a pillar of what the American justice system can be at its most wise, decent, and just.

SOURCES

THE RESEARCH FOR this book involved cross-referencing the many different sources we drew from. These included, chiefly: the transcript of W.D. Lyons's trial and other legal briefs and opinions filed over the course of his case, contemporaneous newspaper reports, and correspondence between the key players in the story from the archives of the NAACP. We also conducted interviews with longtime residents of Choctaw County, some of whom had personal memories of the Lyons case.

Key resources we consulted in the course of our research included, but were not limited to, the following.

Periodicals

Black Dispatch
Chicago Defender
Daily Oklahoman
Hugo Daily News

Museums

Fort Towson Historical Society Museum, Fort Towson, Oklahoma
Tannehill Historical Museum, McAlester, Oklahoma

Books

Baird, W. David, and Danney Goble. *Oklahoma: A History*. Norman: University of Oklahoma Press, 2008.

Bryant, Keith L. Jr. "New Deal," *The Encyclopedia of Oklahoma History and Culture.* www.okhistory.org.

Finkelman, Paul, L. Diane Barnes, Graham Russell Hodges, Gerald Horne, and Cary D. Wintz, eds. *Encyclopedia of African American History, 1896 to the Present: From the Age of Segregation to the Twenty-First Century.* Oxford, UK: Oxford University Press, 2009.

Fisher, Ada Lois Sipuel. *A Matter of Black and White: The Autobiography of Ada Lois Sipuel Fisher.* Norman: University of Oklahoma Press, 1996.

Gibson, Larry S. *Young Thurgood: The Making of a Supreme Court Justice.* Amherst, NY: Prometheus Books, 2012.

King, Gilbert. *Devil in the Grove: Thurgood Marshall, the Groveland Boys, and the Dawn of a New America.* New York: Harper, 2012.

Levy, David W. *The University of Oklahoma: A History, Volume II: 1917–1950.* Norman: University of Oklahoma Press, 2015.

O'Mara, Shane. *Why Torture Doesn't Work: The Neuroscience of Interrogation.* Cambridge, MA: Harvard University Press, 2015.

Reynolds, Dan M. *History of the Oklahoma State Penitentiary 1908–2015.* Oklahoma: Dan M. Reynolds Enterprises, 2017.

Rowan, Carl. *Dream Makers, Dream Breakers: The World of Justice Thurgood Marshall.* New York: Little, Brown, 1993.

Wiegand, Shirley A., and Wayne A. Wiegand. *Books on Trial: Red Scare in the Heartland.* Norman: University of Oklahoma Press, 2007.

Williams, Juan. *Thurgood Marshall: American Revolutionary.* New York: Crown, 1998.

INDEX